Bouquet of Brain Waves

An Extension of Various Ideas, Thoughts,
Imaginations, and Facts

by
Sumathi Kulkarni

Strategic Book Publishing and Rights Co.

Book Design/Layout by Kalpart. Visit
www.kalpart.com

Strategic Book Publishing and Rights Co.
12620 FM 1960, Suite A4-507
Houston TX 77065
www.sbpra.com

ISBN: 978-1-61897-997-1

Dedication

My husband, the late Colonel Rajan Kulkarni, was a gem of a guy who had a pure heart and a compassionate soul. He was a very humble person with a knowledgeable mind. He loved reading and was a voracious reader who developed his own library with the best books from both East and West. His passion for books made him an informed person. His sudden and shocking demise snatched from me his invaluable shower of guidance and encouragement. I would like to pour out my heart and reflect on his selfless love and dedicate this book to my beloved husband.

Foreword

My mother, who wanted me to write instead of taking up a job, my dear husband's encouragement, and my daughter's appreciation of my writing have been the sources of my inspiration, and have worked wonders in boosting my confidence to throw myself wholeheartedly into the art of writing. Though I wrote for school and college magazines, women's magazines, newspapers, *Frozen Thoughts*, and defense magazines, full-fledged writing came only at the tail end of my career.

As the title suggests, this book is a collection of various ideas and innumerable thoughts. It is a bouquet of different narratives full of data, information, facts, and background, not to mention opinion, imagination, judgments, feelings, beliefs, and views.

Sensitivity to animals poured through words, concern for women's freedom through generations flooding out of bondage created by the MCPs (male chauvinistic pigs) of the society, soft, sensitive feelings for the little ones , the future citizens of a nation, the wonderful destinations of travelling minds through the length and breadth of a country, the opening up of education for the underprivileged rural children in various pockets of a nation, a little philosophy on life probably make reading the book better informed, more interesting and is like a plate served with varied delicious items.

A Short Bio

I am a teacher with more than twenty-five years of teaching experience, with a post-graduate degree in English, a post-graduate teaching certificate, and a post-graduate diploma in teaching English from English and Foreign Languages University (EFLU).

A few of my writings have been published in newspapers, *Femina*, *Frozen Thoughts*, and a couple of defense magazines.

I am from a defense background; my husband was a retired colonel. I have a married daughter working in Benguluru.

Acknowledgments

My parents, for providing an intellectual environment.

My bunch of brothers, who served as critics and supporters.

My three sisters-in-law, who unconsciously taught me a lot of little things.

My students, who have been the backbone of my thought process and the flow of ideas for my writing.

My English teacher, without whose contribution to my learning the language I could not have produced this book.

My publishers, who raised my hopes of my book seeing the light of day with minimum investment.

My daughter, who is the source of my energy, dissolves honey into my life, a giver, a giver, and a giver selflessly to all around her.

Lastly, my late husband whose aura I can still feel, whose voice I cannot mistake, who is still an invisible source of strength to my daughter and me.

Table of Contents

Table of Contents

1. Moulding a Child

A baby is a gift of nature. Whether it is a baby plant, a baby animal, or a human baby, it represents God or nature in its purest form. That is why we instantly fall in love with a baby. The baby's nature is ingrained with the quality of growth or development or change. "Change," a natural phenomenon in nature, is continuously struggling to take different forms and shapes. A child grows out of a baby.

A child is a bundle of the finest qualities at the subtlest level. To bring these unmanifest characteristics to their manifestations is a gradual process. A flower blossoms on a plant only in due course of time, under certain care and conditions. Every child needs a mother's love and a father's guidance. Only a guru's blessings can complete it. That is where the importance of teacher arises. The fact that a child takes our attention, energy, time, and a part of our life goes to prove that a teacher's contribution in the development of the child is undeniable.

A child is a symbol of life in its vigorous form. Children are playful and contribute to the spirit in life, children are boundless in thoughts and thus contribute to thinking beyond, children are stress busters, enjoying themselves and making others around them totally involved, which can temporarily help keep away from tension. Children are isolated springs of energy in various colors, hues, and tastes. They pour a lot of positive energy around to make life lighter and easier. It is very acceptable when a teacher views a child's overflowing energy as troublesome and draining. But when the same child comes to you with lot of love, a sorry figure, and an apology without many words, it is a feeling of achievement beyond even Alexander's victory. Loving rewards, strong emotional support, and one-on-one positive rapport works wonders with even the most troublesome children. These are the basic needs, and if provided at the appropriate time and in the right situations, the children are there for everything that a teacher asks for. Then the bother-some situations are rightly controlled on their own. Teaching and the learning process

9

becomes a smooth and enjoyable ride.

A child, whether mischievous or well behaved, is totally focused on the teacher. A sensitive or experienced teacher doesn't miss a chance to bring in any kind of change that is required for the positive development of the child. The rapport is built first and foremost, the rest follows naturally. But how many of us enjoy doing it? And that is supposed to be the essential part of school and the teaching and learning process; academics come later. Once a child settles within the purview of psychological security provided by the teacher it becomes easier, as well as more enjoyable and productive for the teacher. The hurdles dissolve, and the child initiates the learning process and contributes productively. Child-centered teaching and learning dawns and makes learning more fruitful and permanent.

Thus a teacher moulds a child, polishes his or her being, and provides opportunities for emotional and intellectual growth through the years. Once these faculties are irrigated with proper information and knowledge, the child grows in the right direction. The policy of a school should prepare the child with all the skills needed to face the future. Total personality development is a tool that a child carries forward from his or her schooling—confidence, awareness, physique, skills, information, and academics—to be able to lead a life as a complete human being and an aware citizen in the decades to come.

2. Teaching Philosophy

Matru devo bhavah, Pitru devo bhavah, Guru devo bhavah.
Guru Brahma, Guru Vishnu, Guru devo Maheshwara.
Guru sakshat para Brahma, Tasmai shri Guruvennamaha.

The Vedas tell us that immediately after mother and father it is the teacher who takes the place. The teacher is on par with Brahma, Vishnu, and Maheshwara. I bow to him.

A child is a unique creation of nature. A child is like a seed; given rain and sunlight, a plant or tree can grow from fertile land. Nature nurtures it with a lot of invisible care and love. The latest trend in teaching a child without physical or mental abuse effortlessly breeds the warmth of love. Interacting with a child with an engulfing aura of love makes it easy to handle teaching sessions about any information or knowledge.

Mingling with students and creating understanding, a fearless and affectionate rapport, is essential for the perfect exchange of ideas and opinions. It is very necessary that students and their feelings be treated with a sensitive approach. Every child is valued and importance is given to each child. Every child is a unique creation of God. Correcting mistakes without hurting a child's feelings creates a positive rapport between teacher and child.

The teacher's main job as a facilitator is to provide the maximum opportunity for a child to come out with his or her ideas, opinions, suggestions, and questions. Creation of a genuine thirst for knowledge by raising inquiries should be the goal.

Group work and discussions are the best platforms. Fear and shyness should be slowly but surely erased from a child's mind. They are sure blockades in the flow of thought and expression. The technique of physical punishment used in teaching must be discarded. Teaching with love is totally and deeply effective compared to teaching by punishment, which is nasty and nil.

3. The Intricacies of Education

What is today's education all about? This needs a complete analytical approach, keeping in view the changed requirements and expectations of a student in society. In other words, learning should match the needs of society, which is moving at an unimaginable speed to catch up globally. A school that does not fight its way through this will not rightfully survive. To achieve this expectation of the total development of a child, both vertically and laterally, academic and supportive activities are essential. Nevertheless academic highhandedness must be accepted.

The right kind of atmosphere, which ultimately creates an ambience for nurturing a child, must be widespread and involve the right kind of resource persons and resource centers within the institution. Appropriate academic exposure through full-fledged libraries and Internet resources will certainly work wonders.

The growth of a child on all five levels—physical, social, intellectual, emotional, and spiritual—happens during the school years. At this juncture, the role and responsibility of an educational institution is tremendous. This is where the significance of a school is upheld in the society. This responsibility makes its presence felt at every level, from pre-primary to +2 standards. The creation of an appropriate environment is essential for the complete development of the personality of students.

When a teacher provides all levels of information on a given subject or topic, this goes a long way in creating the right approach to learning. Handouts and worksheets work well for drills and practicing a variety of exercises. Any method of making a lesson interesting enhances the probability of attracting the focused attention of wavering minds. These presentations may be either visual or auditory. A teacher's contribution to the facilitating process ultimately builds the confidence of students.

The role of a teacher in building a student's personality throughout the school years—whether it is physical, intellectual, emotional, or spiritual—is very influential. The teacher has to play a role model at every level; the more the sensitivity, the better the role will be.

Value-based learning in school acts as a binding factor in the formation of a strong character. This is like a psychological cushion in facing the ups and downs of life. This is the undercurrent of life that protects a student and boosts as a life skill the ability to handle highs and lows and sail smoothly.

Corporal punishment is the most disputed factor, and legally it should be questioned. It is the most uncivilized way of treating a student in school. It not only hinders a smooth learning process, but could also encourage acquiring and cultivating a negative trend in the character, as the result of a hurt ego. The best way to deal with such a situation is with love and firm counseling, and to keep miles away from physical handling.

A child's thinking process can be encouraged to develop at the primary level. Learning can be 25 percent self-thinking and expression and 75 percent drills, worksheets, and exercises. At the junior level it can be 50–50, and at the senior level one can balance it to 75 percent self-thinking and 25 percent drills and exercises. Under no circumstance should memorization be ignored, as it is an essential part of the mind.

Giving serious thought to the above points and the right implementation on the part of school management will be very beneficial in the long run by providing the best possible student community to society at large.

4. Lifestyle: Relative Value

Indian warriors have been known for their valor, bravery, and gallantry since ancient times. Whether it was the war during the Vedic period, in the times of Ramayana or Mahabharata, during the independence movement, or the recent wars after Independence, the display of heroism has been incredible. Their spirit of love for the motherland is so deep and strong that sacrificing life for the motherland is as natural as any other emotion. The young and the brave in Indian history have displayed this emotion with perfection and have laid down their lives for our country.

I was very proud to be the wife of a man in uniform. One morning, my husband told me that we had to go to a party organized in the honor of an officer who had just joined. It was a quiet and pleasant evening. I wondered throughout the party what was it about this new officer that made him stand out. He talked to everyone at the party, but was classically a person who did not speak much. He looked like a perfect gentleman, with an impressive aura around him. He seemed to have all the values of a good soldier.

When we returned home, I told my husband about my impressions. He listened and quickly added, "Yes, he is also a winner of the peacetime award Shaurya Chakra" (an honorable decoration for an Indian soldier). I had heard of war heroes, soldiers decorated for their action in war and during times of peace, so I was curious to know about the story behind this honor. This is how I heard it from my husband.

This officer was traveling with his wife and his children to the place where he was posted. The train was moving through a disturbed area in the northwestern part of the country. Suddenly, the train stopped at a station. Within few minutes, a group of hired miscreants (*goondas*) came with rods and chains and started beating the terrified passengers. Nobody dared to take them on. The officer didn't know what was happening. When asked a police sub-inspector and two constables came to the officer with information and told him about the situation. The hired miscreants were on the platform. Some tried to burn the bogey (compartment of a long train). Seeing the flames, the officer grabbed the police inspector's weapon and hurled a couple of rounds at the miscreants, overpowering them. He was now in control of the situation. The culprits were caught and handed over to the police, who by then had arrived more in greater number. Everything was under control. There was a sudden lull and then peace at the station.

Later, the District Magistrate, the district Superintendent of Police, and other officials came to the station and took the details of the situation and the details of the officer. They thanked him profusely. Six hours later, the train again began its journey to its destination.

The officer forgot about the incident and got involved in his daily routine as a soldier. Then, one fine day, he was informed that he was being honored with Shaurya Chakra for his show of valor and gallantry in peacetime. Normally, the decision to give this award is decided and offered by the top brass of the army. This was a special case in which the report and award recommendation were prepared by the District Magistrate, the Superintendent of Police, and the Collector.

We rarely meet such real-life heroes in our lives. We read about them and see them on screen, but seldom meet them. I was privileged to meet a hero who risked his own life to save his fellow travelers. India has born such people throughout its past and present, and this trend of pride will certainly continue in the future. This is a country with a heart and feelings, and emotions are displayed wholeheartedly whenever necessary.

5. The Last Journey

You know something,
I also was in a living form
Like you all with a caring mother
And a mini herd of siblings.
My mom made sure that I grew out
To be fat, plump, and biggest of all the piglets.
Me being proud of my size
Turned out to be a curse.
The devil in the form of man
With his friends chased, cornered, and
Tied me mercilessly
To their vehicle, upside down.
It was fear turned to terror,
It was dusk turning to dark night,
It was the worst and the last journey of my life.
I was separated from my family.
My siblings scattered in terror.
But I could read my mother's mind
In her eyes, she huddled in a corner
As I was hanging
Perhaps she knew my destiny of dark hell.
It was cruel misery
As I reached darkest night
When my soul was separated from my body
By those butchers called "Men."
The last spark that passed through me was
The flash I saw in my mother's eyes
She cursed the men with the same
Kind of death as mine.
How can I make man realize
Ahimsa is the way to peace and bliss?

6. The Position of the English Language in India

English, as we all know, is a language of Britain that traveled to India along with British traders who succeeded over all other European traders who wanted to establish themselves in India. Britain not only made commercial gains, but found Indian society full of superstitions that could easily be socially dominated. Its main representative, the East India Company, played a pivotal role in introducing English as the language taught in schools. This was the potential turning point that nurtured the deeper roots of Indian society. So it was, and the use of English is still growing day by day to reach its current state.

People support this, as it not only serves as a common language among Indian states and citizens, but also provides a global language for professionals with an extra dream. To achieve their goal, and be accepted globally, they have to learn English.

The culture in India is going through a transitional phase. People who are ambitious and desire economic prosperity want to learn English and imitate Western culture, even at the cost of their indigenous languages and cultures. The spread of education is growing fast, and the rural population doesn't want to be left behind in this race of perfecting the English language. There is widespread learning of English, even in rural areas. This positive sign is welcome, but in the bargain learning our own languages has slid down to a minimum throughout the entire country. This is a sad state of affairs. Where is this going to lead us? Future generations may completely lose touch, which could result in the death of our languages, and ultimately our culture. Now is the time for all the intellectuals in India to come together and save our ancient culture and rich heritage. I feel that we should maintain a balance by accepting English and embracing our existing rich culture. We gained our independence half a century ago, and cannot allow our culture to fade away in the bright light of British domination.

At times I feel that this kind of fear is baseless. Considering that our culture and civilization is thousands of years of old, it is quite strong enough to accept the positive aspects of change and filter out negative influences, and become much stronger in the process. India was probably dominated by the British because we were not united as one single unit; we were involved in fights among ourselves and engulfed in deep-rooted superstitions. On the other hand British gave us back a strong union—our country. They gave us a common language; eradicated many social evils, such as *sati* (the religious practice of self-immolation on the funeral pyre by the widow of the deceased); and encouraged widow remarriages through regulations. We were enlightened through various means, and unlike the proverb of "frog in the well" we now see and participate in the global world.

The English language has served as a window to the world. It has brought India quite a few Nobel Prize winners in various disciplines—Rabindranath Tagore, C. V. Raman, Amartya Sen, and others. English has led innumerable intellectuals from India to the latest wonder (i.e., computers). People from India are not only contributing to global prosperity, but are returning to their roots and trying to eradicate poverty in their home country.

I feel strongly that we must pursue the English language and explore the opportunities it brings, but also simultaneously revere and work toward developing our own languages and culture with equal zeal and zest. Every language of India has a rich and varied literature contributed by local and regional intellectuals, and this cannot be ignored. It has to be valued, translated, and presented globally.

Humans are naturally attracted to economic prosperity, and learning English in the present time will certainly lead one to greener pastures. Instead of accepting the idea that this will give way to the slow and steady death of our languages and culture, I remain optimistic about the further blossoming of our culture. There is an ocean of knowledge in the Vedas (holy Hindu scriptures), and many areas of the Vedas are explored by scholars, who make them accessible to people locally, nationally, and globally. If we allow this to cease, we will be at a tremendous loss. I think this should not and cannot happen. The West is hungry to know the deeper layers of Vedic knowledge. Both regional languages and Sanskrit, mother of all Indian languages, are necessary to understand the Vedas.

In the present scenario, English stands as the essential medium for the exchange of ideas and gives an impetus for progress. It provides challenges to compete and grow, as well as various avenues for further development, but it also ensures economic and financial progress that will lead to prosperity. India is already a potentially powerful country in the Asian subcontinent and could even become one of the superpowers.

The invention of the computer and its fast development is one of the essential achievements of present times. The contribution of Indian brains to the computer world is indisputable. The Indian brain is recognized as one of the finest. This is made possible by the English language, which provides a strong medium of communication throughout the world.

7. My Freedom

My conscience is my inner self,
It is the best of my friends,
I always chat with it,
It is always sincere,
It is the best guide,
I confide in it most of the time,
I share my happiness with it,
I go to it in my difficult times,
It is the most reliable,
It is the most truthful,
It solves my conflicts,
It is always right,
I surrender to what is right,
And that is my freedom.

8. The Highway

Cows, bulls, buffaloes, big and small,

Herded through the highway,

I wonder what for,

Putting a break on the vehicle,

A simultaneous break on my thinking, with a closer look, a horrible sight,

The herd was ill fed,

At the end of a careless and gruesome truck journey,

Probably a few hundred miles,

Some sick, some wounded with

Exposed blood, stained skin,

Forced to walk, bear the brunt

Of cruel beating to reach the destination,

Unknown to the ignorant souls.

But then, they are taken to the butcher

For slaughtering

By the most sensitive species of the planet

"The Man"!

9. Futile Screech

What am I seeing in the sky?
Crows, not one, not two, but many flying high,
Loss of comfort, rise of misery,
Their hearts screeching to the upcoming cruelty,
The whole flock is restless
To the discomfort, could not express,
But who is listening,
All cries subdued in one's own noise,
The noise of the most evolved species
Serving his selfish purpose
By felling the tree, felling
The nests of the crows.
The huge tree that selflessly supported
Innumerable species for ages
Falls like a helpless giant in the hands of
The most sensitive species of the planet
"The Man"!

10. My Role as an English Teacher

Today I can boast of having about twenty-five years of experience teaching the English language. Every year of my experience has enriched me with better ways and means of teaching, and this is highly satisfying. When I look back at my first year of teaching, I certainly feel I have come a long way in enriching my knowledge of the language and enhancing my skills. This doesn't mean anything other than the fact that I still have a long way to go.

Rather than teaching at only one school, I have taught in different schools in the different states of India. This was not only challenging, it was also enjoyable. Every place has its own level of education and level of English as a second language. The higher the level of education the more enjoyable the teaching; teaching is more challenging if the level of education is lower. Either way it is a learning experience for the teacher.

Depending on the requirement of the school, I had the opportunity to teach at the primary level up through the +2 or intermediate levels. Teaching is different at every level. When one gets addicted to teaching, one enjoys teaching and creates a meaningful rapport with the students regardless of their IQ level.

There are three types of educational systems in our country i.e. ICSE (Indian Certificate for School Education), ISC (Indian School Certificate), CBSE (Central Board of Secondary Education) and SSB (State Secondary Board - The state apex organisation of education for secondary school examinations). I had the chance to teach in different schools that followed different systems. The ultimate objective of all three systems is the same, i.e., to learn English as a life skill for the purpose of communication. There are, however, differences among the three systems. The ICSE stresses English as a subject that initiates the thinking process, creativity, and original expression. The CBSE is communication oriented. The State Board (SSB) dishes out English to the students, making it comparatively easy and simple.

Reading, recitation at junior and senior levels, and rhymes at pre-primary and primary levels are essential for correct pronunciation and verbal expression. This is an important aspect that needs to be stressed in the classroom. Reading lessons, reciting poems, and role playing go a long way in achieving the proper use of the English language.

In writing, the primary skills taught are spelling, punctuation, legible handwriting, and correct sentence structure. At the primary level, a watch on handwriting is essential, followed by spelling, and then on to simple sentences. Teaching proper grammar is essential. Fewer mistakes will be made if the student's knowledge of grammar is in place. To enhance writing skills among students, the best way is to use self-prepared worksheets. These can be used heavily throughout the year at both primary and junior levels.

The third important skill is that of listening. This is how a student is taught to understand what he/she reads. Reading has no purpose without understanding. The best way to teach this skill is by working with comprehension passages, which English teachers normally do. Preparing or picking out passages, followed by questions, giving them as handouts, works wonders. With practice the learning process becomes easier.

The last skill is conversational speech. English is a foreign language to the majority of students. Initially it is very difficult for a student to learn, particularly if they are from a rural and illiterate background. Students suffer a loss of confidence and low self-esteem. Tackling this at the primary level is the most practical method. Good English teachers, as well as exposure to audio recordings and videos, are important, as they will acquaint the student with proper pronunciation. Encouraging students to participate in different forums will help.

Overall, clarity of expression, brevity, and accuracy are looked at in both written and spoken language. Stressing these aspects in a right and timely manner will go a long way in improving the quality of English language taught in schools.

Apart from organizing and conducting literary-based activities, running an English club that involves poetry recitation, role playing, enacting plays or dramas, and holding creative writing competitions for poetry, plays, and essays would enhance, enrich, and strengthen students' language skills.

In summary, I have been using all the methods mentioned above, and have been successful in teaching English as a common, global language at various levels of education. I have been teaching students to develop all four skills so that they can meet their day-to-day requirements, and it certainly works.

11. Wings of Imagination

Imagination, one of the faculties of the mind, is so vast that only the sky is the limit. As a girl, Charu was frequented with kindled imagination. She questioned herself—"why do only birds fly? Why not people?" Her creativity flared up. She thought of artificial wings. Instead of going to the market or school on a bicycle or scooter, why not fly with wings? Little Charu thought of having different kinds and different sizes wings for different people.

How nice the sky would look if people reached their destinations that way instead of by roads.

"Charu, where are you? Why don't you come and help me?" Charu's mother asked from the kitchen.

"Yes mamma, I'll come," Charu answered.

In spite of this interruption, her imagination would continue with its wings. "How nice it would be if we flew to school in groups. Oh! I am thrilled at the thought," she thought to herself. She would cry when she saw cranes flying in flocks. There would be rush hour in the sky, traffic jams, and accidents. "Oh God! That would be terrible," she sighed. But it would be exciting, adventurous, and time saving. Of all the boons it would provide, the best would be the reduction of traffic jams on roads.

Why shouldn't the technology develop in this direction? It would be fantastic!

12. The Morning Sunshine

The morning sunshine,
Will it ever be mine?
I have a dream
To be counted in the cream
I have a dream
To be the finest forever and ever green.
I have a dream
To go beyond the sky and reach the stars.
I have a dream
To fulfill it even beyond any stars.
I have a dream
To make the sunshine past of mine.
Can I reach the morning sunshine?!!!!!

13. The Day I Sprouted...

The day I sprouted
I saw a big and wide world lying around
And was awed.
I embraced the sunshine
As my lips pouted.
Growing inch by inch I matured,
I had many friends
With a bounty of will.
We all grew to be bigger and larger
And stronger at ends.
May be two or three years passed by
I would now see the horizon,
Feel the wind and
Welcome the almighty sun.
One day, as it happened,
I saw a figure completely tired and stunned.
He came to me, his deep blue eyes
Expressed a world, his world.
He sat at my foot
And closed his deep blue troubled eyes,
With relief.
The contentment I saw
In those deep blue eyes
When they opened overwhelmed me.
The joy of just being there
And still helping was incredible.
He got up, turned to look at me,
The beautiful blue eyes stared silently at me.

There was something missing in them
What I saw was the glitter of a gem.
That night, it felt long,
But when dawn came, it
Sent an unknown shiver.
Suddenly I heard a noise screaming
Through the breeze
What I saw made me freeze.
I heard the pain, agony of my friends.
They were being torn down
The horror of it all let the warmth of sunlight,
The cool breeze, the calmness of my world drown.
There was sudden silence,
I saw a deathbed, I saw pain
I saw my friends slain
I saw anguish, I saw fear,
I saw the dark blue eyes again.

14. Examination Blues

To understand examination blues, we need to understand the purpose of exams. The purpose of exams is not to create fear among those who write them, but to understand how much knowledge has been absorbed and understood, and if a person's ability has increased. This fear is caused in students by the misunderstanding that the purpose of exams is obtaining good marks. This lack of understanding is present in the majority of today's parents as well. The victim is obviously the student.

Why do examination blues occur? A simple answer is insufficient and inappropriate study. Perhaps those who are blessed with an unbounded memory are those capable of obtaining high marks with distinction. Sadly, our examination system tests only the memory. God's plan is different. He has made each one of us unique and not every person can score marks with distinction. It is as simple as that. The pressure of the vast syllabus, the high expectations of parents and schools, and uncertainty about meeting those expectations are some of the causes of this fear of exams. The question is, what is more important, good marks or the understanding and application of knowledge? In many cases marks do not guarantee a student's capability. Yet they are the indicators. How can this be balanced?

When it comes to exam time, exams are the cause of nervousness, sweating, rapid heartbeat, confusion, memory loss, unorganized presentation, and more. In extreme cases, they can cause suicidal tendencies. Nature has given us the power of overcoming these problems and emerging victorious in the majority of cases. As students we all go through these experiences, and the best part is that we are all sailing in the same boat. That is a heartening part of it, the feeling of not being the only one on the journey. This feeling brings warmth, confidence, hard work, and the right kind of attitude toward preparation for the exam. When it comes to tackling fear, the role played by the parents, the school, the state, and the teacher is very important. They can provide support for the student's study and hard work, acting like pillars of strength and confidence. Having a friendly attitude is essential to smooth communication with children. Having a balanced approach when it comes to health, studies, and games and entertainment, with a focused attention toward studies that stresses the importance of intense and passionate hard work, will certainly take children in the right direction.

Each party has a role in taking responsibility for the concerned child; when this occurs, the impact is automatically created. The state and its agencies should create policies that are relevant, practical, and helpful to students at the high school and professional levels. In this process, apoliticization of the concerned agencies is essential and cannot be ruled out.

Children are at school most of their student life. Keeping this in mind, it is necessary that the school take care of the students in their educational areas. These include physical, emotional, social, moral, spiritual, aesthetic, and ethical developments. The school can also program itself to increase the number of examinations and tests throughout the year. Psychologically, the more you face a situation, the less you fear it. This applies to examinations. The more a student appears for examinations, the easier it becomes to take them.

The next important element is the role of the parents. They are like the foundation of a monument. If they are strong then the chances of making an error in bringing up their child are minimal. Lastly, a teacher's support for students who appear to take examinations works like a miracle in reducing the examination blues.

A student must have a genuine and burning desire to do well on the examinations. A positive attitude certainly helps. With support and encouragement, students can bring a cooler attitude toward examinations, thereby converting the examination blues to pleasant greens.

15. The Art of Marriage

A good marriage must be created.

In marriage the little things are the big things.

It is never too old to hold hands.

It is never going to sleep angry.

It is having a mutual sense of values and common objectives.

It is standing together facing the world.

It is forming a circle of love that gathers the whole family.

It is speaking words of appreciation and demonstrating
gratitude in thoughtful ways.

It is having the capacity to forgive and forget.

It is giving each other an atmosphere in which each can grow.

It is not only marrying the right person, it is being the right
person.

16. Why Telangana? A Perspective

It is absolutely ignorant to say that the Telangana agitation is created by media. It has been prevalent from the time of independence, took its ugliest turn in 1969–70, when it was thoroughly, and with a stern hand, curbed by the then chief minister Brahmananda Reddy. Prime Minister Indira Gandhi tried to solve the problem with a six-point formula within the framework of Andhra Pradesh by making a Telangana leader, Marri Chenna Reddy, the chief minister. Unfortunately, this formula was twisted to the extent that it was not implemented in toto. It was made suitable and favorable to the Andhras. As a result, the fifteen-year domicile was brought down to four years and was called a local candidate certificate. This was a slap in the face of Telangana, as the opportunities for admissions to universities and government employment were lost for the next forty years, and it is still the same today. All the outsiders calling themselves local candidates made a fortune for themselves at the cost of the Telanganites.

It is a sad story that the Telugu are considered downtrodden in their own region. This goes back to the seven generations of Muslim rule that made them slaves in their own homes, followed by the British domination that left the Telanganites nowhere. Now the rulers don't want to leave Hyderabad as they have made it a heaven for themselves in making money. The prosperity lies with the Andhras, and they have grabbed education and university seats by twisting the government rules in their favor. They do not leave a single opportunity to suppress the Telanganites and that too working democratically because they have a majority in the legislative assembly!!

Hyderabad! Hyderabad! Hyderabad! The city is located almost in the center of the region. Geographically it belongs only to this region. All the structures that are found here were built by past rulers using the resources of the Telangana people and their region. Only the Telanganites have the right to claim the city. Who has built the famous Charminar monument and with what resources? Osmania University, Osmania Hospital, Tank Bund, Nizam's Institute of Medical Sciences, the majestic Residency that now houses Osmania University College for Women, and the Legislative Assembly were all built by the money and labor of the people of this region.

The high-tech city has a cosmopolitan culture that comes from business and development, and is not identified with any particular people. There are business houses that have contributed from all corners of India. Employees have poured in from every part of India and are working toward national development. If one talks about the overpasses and the national highways that cross the region, that is a part of the competitive lateral development of all cities in India that are striving to develop and grow. The International Airport is a unique imitation of international standards built at the expense of city people, bringing them only inconvenience. The facility providers make the best of their income by taxing the people. Most of the latest malls, jewelry outlets, hospitals, and most modern schools are nothing but commercially oriented, money-centered organizations that are interested in making themselves rich in the name of development.

Land that is acquired from the government by Seemandhra business people for any development or business activities in and around the twin cities of Hyderabad is public property. Though they have invested the money the land belongs to the Telangana region. No one can claim it is owned by anyone.

People living in the districts of Telangana have schools without proper teachers, a couple of universities without the required standards, and hospitals without specialists and appropriate equipments. For all these basic necessities they have to run to Hyderabad, and those who can't afford to leave themselves to fate. The people of Telangana are ignored and dominated by outsiders. If they rise to rebel for their constitutional right to freedom where will the fault lie? Any government may suppress the Telangana but will never win over them. This issue will arise repeatedly in the coming times.

The unwillingness of the state to take a dynamic step and declare Telangana a separate state shows the incompetency of the Central Government. Telanganites have the birth right to rule themselves after seven hundred years of continuous suppression, first Muslim, then British, and now Andhra. This is a legitimate demand. Andhras have proven over the last six decades that they are ruling with utterly selfish interest. Otherwise this problem would never have occurred. The root cause of the problem lies with the misrule of Andhras. Separate them into two states and things will fall into place.

Nothing much has been done by Andhra to develop Hyderabad as they have claimed. It was a city with all the requirements for a capital and it remains the same. All structures were already established before they thronged the city few decades back. In the high-tech city, the companies belong to outsiders. The land provided to these companies by the Andhra government belongs to Telangana. Andhras have established businesses and are making money at the cost of the Telangana people. Is that development? Surely not.

This region belongs to the Telangana people, and the Andhras should not decide anything for it. They can talk about their own region but cannot thrust the Samaikya Andhra Movement on Telanganites. How can they fight with the rights of Telangana? They can only plead and if they are not heard then they have to go back to their own region. They cannot in any way encroach on the rights of the Telangana people who want to rule their own region. It is sheer audacity of the Andhras to make decisions about somebody else's land. This is not right and cannot be accepted. How will they shed the sweetness of power that they have tasted for more than six decades? The Telangana people will have to work very hard to be released from the clutches of power-hungry Andhra politicians.

By allowing them to rule themselves, the problem will be solved. There will be peace and harmony in all areas.

17. A View on the Srikrishna Committee

The Srikrishna Committee has not understood the Telangana issue in toto and is biased. It is not an emotional issue as the report stated. This is the result of the biased rule of the Andhra government since its inception in 1956. All the options recommended by the committee have been tried and have failed miserably due to the self centered attitude of Andhra rulers. You cannot equate the shrewd, tactful, and deft Andhras with the simple, straightforward, and impulsive people of Telangana. The Andhras have had the chance to develop and grow while the Telanganites have faced suppression throughout the last seven hundred years of history, first by the Muslim, then the British, and now the Andhras. They have not tasted real independence at all. Therefore, it is not an emotional issue. They crave their independence.

It is ironic that history is being repeated. There is a deliberate creation of pressure on the suppression of the people's genuine demands. Srikrishna is an outsider to the state; he cannot fully understand the issue and is certainly under the shrewd influence of the Andhra policy of suppression. This is a democracy where the e-media and print media cannot be banned from talking about these issues. We have a right to information. "Unless handled deftly, tactfully and firmly as discussed under option six," states the committee's report. What does this mean? Suppress their demand by using force and killing and not let the people know about it? Or find a new way to do the same? Is it talking about continuing autocratic rule as the Andhra have ruled since 1956? Where is the right to expression and right to information? This is a very sad state of affairs coming from a committee that is supposed to be thorough and professional. The secret document, submitted to the government is another feather in the cap of the Srikrishna Committee's misadventure.[1]

---

[1] Srikrishna Committee was formed to assess Telangana issue and give its recommendations. Secret document is a part of recommendations that was not made public.

18. An Exhausted Soul but a Contented Spirit

It is something beautiful to marry a soldier and feel that one belongs to the family of the armed forces, and to feel that one is a part of serving the motherland, though in an indirect way. That life has its highs and lows, and its bright and dark sides. For me, it was a roller coaster journey. Sometimes it was a lot of fun and other times it was tough lonely life that taught me how to be independent and self-reliant. It had its own perks, much better than what the MNCs (Multi National Comapanies) offer today. It gave me the opportunity to move from the western range of the Himalayas to the eastern range, and move up to the southern tip where the oceans meet.

It was just like the life of the Banjaras. We had to move at short notice and be efficient in providing for ourselves. Our requirements included food, clothing, and shelter, along with the children's necessities. We moved by air, by road, and by train. In special times we moved by special trains, by which I mean the whole unit moved with their families. This was a really pleasurable occurrence to remember and cherish. Those who love traveling are blessed and I am one of them. It is heartening to recollect the visits to all types of terrain with various topographic expressions: the mountains like a guard picketing our borders, the restless shores, the sprawling plains, the dense and extensive jungles. Nature in all its beauty has stayed with me as a haunting treasure.

Each region of India has its own special cuisine. One should be fortunate enough to get a chance to taste these varieties from different regions. I believe I was one of those lucky ones. Kashmiri *waza*, Punjabi *dana* (food); Delhi's varieties of *dudh malai*; *sandesh* or *rosgolla* of Bengal; Rajasthani sweets; *sambar* and *rasam*, *idli* and *dosa* from the southern states; there is no end to it. Every food from every corner of India is unique in terms of taste and delicacies. Even TV programs on food cannot make one feel the real experience of what I am writing about. Only the genuine experience can give this understanding.

There is another side that is not as attractive, but the moment it is overcome, it brings out the best of you. There are days when you must temporarily face life on your own. One has no option but to face it supported by the suggestions and guidance needed to complete the required tasks, whether these task are about you, your children, or managing one's finances. This makes you completely capable of dealing with yourself, your fears, and your confidence. Fear is dissolved into and replaced with confidence. What is worse is when the situation becomes a permanent one. I have seen my friends face such circumstances with grit and determination, facing life alone with a positive attitude and moving forward. I not only pray for them but also wish them well. Sometimes there is wavering patriotism in the face of separation and death.

Growing strong and tough from within seems to be an inevitable process. That is why there is always an edge in the personalities of the wives and children of defense personnel over civilians. What we have in us is time-tested confidence, self-assurance, poise, self-belief, self-reliance, buoyancy, resilience, optimism, cheerfulness, good spirits, enthusiasm, and coolness, to name a few qualities. All of these qualities build the inner strength to positively move forward in life. When one's environment is influenced by strict discipline, it affects the spontaneous cultivation of discipline within, which manifests itself in the outside world. This unconsciously cultivated discipline takes us much further than others in everything we do. This is a unique, exceptional, and exclusive way of living that is dedicated to a life committed to one's country.

It is a complete package of life's learning in every area of life's activities. Acquiring knowledge, inculcating discipline, learning about reality, being exposed to various lands and cultures in India, along with extensive travel and spontaneous learning leads to the rise of confidence and knowledge. Is there an educational institution that provides all of these on one platform while remaining within the family? No, there isn't? But it does exist. The family of defense personnel in the armed forces! Surprised? Don't be. The above write-up is accountable to my statement.

After spending thirty-three years of his precious life in the service of the nation, the Almighty blessed me with the return of my husband. In the tail end of life there is peace and satisfaction. By retirement the exhausted soul finds salvation in the contentment of the spirit with the feeling that in some way one was useful in serving of the nation with commitment, dedication, and patriotism.

19. Sikkimese Splendor

Being married to defense personnel means the opportunity to visit various places. As I was one of those lucky ones I had the chance to visit Sikkim and get acquainted with its lovely people, the women in particular. Small but beautiful, Sikkim is situated in the eastern Himalayas. It is spread below Mount Kanchendzonga (28,225 ft), the third highest peak in the world, and revered by the Sikkimese as their "protective deity."

Amid the grandeur of the mountain peaks, lush valleys, fast-flowing rivers, and terraced hills, Sikkim offers a rare and singular experience. Much more beautiful than the natural surroundings are the Asian-featured, plump-cheeked, soft-skinned, and bright-complexioned women. The boys and girls mix freely and often end up marrying. Three main groups of people make up the population of Sikkim, the Lepchas, the Bhutias, and the Nepalese. Sikkimese women are simple, polite, and non-aggressive, with a natural gaiety. *Baku*, a two-piece dress worn by the Lepcha and Bhutia girls, makes them look even more attractive and enhances their beauty.

Who says women are backward and suppressed? The age-old civilization of Sikkim has seen nothing but matriarchal families where the woman is the head of the family. She makes the decisions and works for their livelihood. She runs the business, and looks after the cattle and land in a broader sense. In Gangtok, the capital of Sikkim, women have taken jobs in schools.

Just like their menfolk, the women are also devoted to Buddhism. One finds monasteries (*gompa*) in every part of this land. One of these is the Rumtek Monastery, which has a huge statue of Lord Buddha. It is situated about 17 miles from the capital. North Sikkim has its own splendor with a popular hot spring. East Sikkim has sprawling lakes on its mountains.

If provided with the proper education and environment, women's potential can be increased for their own betterment.

20. Lady, Graduate Yourself!

Would you like to do everything at one time? Beg your pardon; you say it's not possible? You see, nothing is impossible. That is what one learns here.

The first month is busy, with the husband settling down at the college, the children settling down at school, the lady settling into the new accommodation that has all the ready-made facilities available but is not without the shadowy music of whining.

Once the momentum of keeping busy picks up, then in every home there is a busy lady. At every turn you find a lady walking, waiting for the bus, driving mopeds, scooters, and cars. They have started to look busy.

The officers go about their work, and the ladies are free to do anything. To go riding and join the hunt club (never mind if a couple of bones get broken, they will always heal), to become professionals in beauty care, to master computers at the computer club, to try their hand at painting and decoupage, and don't leave out the most interesting, to try their ability at cooking and baking. "The way to a man's heart is through his stomach," as the proverb goes. In this respect, Selveraj, the cook, is a boon. There is also the possibility to learn driving in the hills and become more confident to drive ahead in life. Don't forget croquet and golf for those who are interested.

Ladies practice for the section wise entertainment for the ladies club. One sees potential DSSC (Defence Services Staff College) queens, Navy queens, moving around busily on this Queen of the Hills![2]

The more the officers are loaded with studies, the busier the ladies are. One can find a lady attending so many activities other than the frequent syndicate and regimental get-togethers

---

[2] The hill station in TamilNadu state of India is called Ootacamund (Ooty in short) where soldier officer's course is conducted. It is called **'The Queen of Hills'** for its nature's beauty.

that half of one's time is spent training the maid, who is the only source of help around. If you don't lose one or can't find one then you are lost until the end of the course. It is a stepping stone indeed, to learn to become more and more independent.

The course is a tough one. At every step, each competition is a test. In computers there is a test every two weeks. Children have frequent tests. Either you study or you teach your children. This simply means that either you pass the test or your child does. The choice is very clear. If both pass it is an achievement that really needs celebration.

A very practical, useful, and informative course is the institutionalized training for officer's wives, it is given to make us a better component of our organization. Covering money matters, health, education, etiquette, behavioral science, and more, it is an intellectual combination of all subjects, and is an excellent boost to one's personality.

Visit all the places of interest in the nearby states like Mysore, Rameshwaram, Tirupathi, and Mudhumalai during breaks or go to a holiday resort for a change. That should keep you fit in a different way altogether.

For those who are interested in social welfare activities there are old-age homes and plantation programs. Quite a few ladies enjoy going out of their way to get into such activities. You are training to learn to live a fulfilling life by getting involved in various ways.

The best part of this experience is that you live without knowing where you will be going in a couple months. You are caught unaware when you get your posting orders. Then there are packing pains, your husband's studies, the children's examinations, and to top it all off, a computer exam if one is really up for it! One is grateful to the Almighty if she gets through all this without losing her mental balance. Once you are finished the sense of achievement is unbelievable.

To vent your saturated feelings, the provision of "the owl" exists. This exercise flushes out all frustrations through the pen. Using creativity in this way lightens your mood and keeps your senses sharp so that you are able to laugh at yourself and enjoy life.

After ten months, you will have graduated from your

DSSC stay. A very fruitful experience, and a rewarding one for those who take it.

"I came, I saw, I conquered," as Julius Caesar said. That's it!

However, for this challenge a lady must be properly qualified. She needs to have a husband who has been selected for DSSC. I wish every lady the opportunity to have this wonderful, sweet-and-sour chili sauce experience.

21. Life

Life, love, seek, home, help, hope. Do you find any similarity in these words? I know all these words have the letter "e" in them, but try harder.

These words are principles for our existence. Life is a four-letter word but we sometimes do not pay attention to it. It's a common misconception that life means living but it's absolutely untrue. Life is not just living, it's the art of living. It's not just a period of time that you are on earth, it is how much time you have utilized and how much you have benefited others.

Life is the art of drawing an eraser. Once past, time is gone forever and cannot come back. Life starts as a single cell, be it a plant or an animal or a fungi. Life begins when an individual is separated from the mother and leads his or her own life. Nobody can ever define "life."

We think that food, clothing, and shelter are essential to life, but love, hope, and prayer also help. Just think about it! To live a successful life, make your mind a cool factory, your body a steel factory, and your tongue a sweet factory.

We should try to have healthy relationships with others. In this world of fast food and fast lives people seldom have time for each other. Take time from your profession for your parents, family, and friends because that is the successful way of living life.

Everyone lives for himself or herself. What if you are only one among the crowd? Be an individual and have your own separate identity even if you are in the crowd. Live for others like the trees, rivers, and flowers. Try to be different in your own way. Let no one deceive you.

Eat for need, not for greed. Diseases are taxes paid for your pleasures. Stop paying them. Be calm and maintain tranquility. No one should waver from their right path. The snakes are poisonous and the sandalwood tree is full of pleasant fragrance and aroma. Our best efforts could be to spread smiles on every face where there is a frown.

We need to live life judiciously, but on our own terms. Understand duties first and then demand your rights. Why act as a worm and blame others for stepping on you? Never bow your head unless you have committed a mistake. Do not expect anything from anyone because expectations lead to frustrations. Be sweet-tempered to everyone you meet. Anger leads to many complications in life. Give happiness to everybody because happiness grows by sharing. Share in sorrow as sorrow decreases by sharing. Life means loving your friends and foes equally and immensely.

22. Women of Substance

Grandmother

She belonged to the early twentieth century. She married at the age of thirteen. A naive young girl with a wheat-colored complexion and big doe eyes, attired as a bride in a nine-yard silk sari. She struggled to carry the unmanageable, flowing garment, a real sight to see for all who had come for the marriage. She was continuously supported and helped by all, especially her mother. She wondered what exactly was happening as her happiness extended to her new clothes and jewelry. Her excitement was limited to sharing new things with her friends, who were as innocent and childlike as she was. She was not bothered about her bridegroom, a tall, fair, strong, and handsome man around thirty years old. None of that mattered to her because she was completely unaware of what marriage was all about.

In those days girls were married when they reached puberty or often even before. A girl used to be living in her in-laws house before she knew anything about life in general and her life in particular. Grandmother would say, "He loved me a lot. By the time I could understand my marriage I had my first child. And this continued, it became a routine, every alternate year my family grew by one member. I had no free time, in fact I had no time at all as I was busy with a new arrival every other year. But I was very happy as he respected, cared, and loved me." Her mother interpreted this as his overflowing love for her daughter. She said this because he was not happy with his first wife, as she was mentally unstable. He was rich, educated, and a graduate, belonging to a higher caste Brahmin family and he was also blessed with a large dowry from his first wife. Richness was not a problem, but nobody would dare to give their daughter to a secondhand bridegroom. "But my case was different," grandmother would say. "When he came to know that my father, who was a Pujari in Tuljabhavani Temple, was drowned in debts, and that he had married his two daughters but was left with the youngest one still to be married, he offered to clear all my father's debts in return for his marriage to me." She swelled with pride while narrating the story of her marriage, something like a fairytale.

This divine physical love produced a dozen children until she began having problems in her forties, and her overworked uterus was removed under the guidance of a city doctor. Surprisingly, there were no parenting problems. Her children grew on their own in a natural atmosphere, they were all ingrained with honesty, integrity, education, and hard work by their exemplary father, who was their idol and was followed with respect. Then prosperity was transformed into poverty as the family head was a teacher in a government school and it was difficult to provide basic necessities for the growing children. Her daughters were married off on a first-come, first-served basis. Having choices, desires, and wishes was a distant dream for these six girls. They either were not aware of them or everything was gulped away in the poverty stricken, unsupportive environment that influenced their way of life. In other words, they simply had to kill their feelings and emotions. The sons graduated from school, unlike their female siblings, and left home to fend for themselves. To make both ends meet, her husband had to work even after retirement and succumbed to a lonely death at a school in a far off place.

This caused upheaval in grandmother's life. She was literally uneducated, mentally unaware of the world outside that she had not been exposed to until now, and physically exhausted after producing a dozen healthy children. Losing her life support emotionally, physically, mentally, financially, and socially was a cumbersome task for her, but life teaches everything and necessity makes one learn all. She became strong and moved ahead in life. She went to schools and colleges in her nine-yard sari to gain admission for her children. Slowly and steadily she moved to the city where she could get some support from her married daughters. Within no time she had learned a lot and became accustomed to city life. She enjoyed movies in the theaters, even and the English ones that were popular. As a lady in her fifties with her children settled in various directions, she was a content, with only intermittent sad memories of her husband, who had been like a divine light in the darkness of her father's poverty-stricken home.

It was amazing hear the evolution of a typical village girl into a city-living grandmother with an open mind and love of freedom. Adjusting to the changing times, mingling with all sorts of crowds, and being one with them is not as easy as one might think. But necessity teaches all. She knew the tricks of the trade and was at ease with her teenaged grandchildren as much as she was with people her own age. She had a dynamic personality and was always there for the celebrations and grief of her twelve children, and that kept her continuously occupied throughout her life. She never lost her heart at anything, she was a woman made of steel, full of courage, and flexible to no end.

Change is the law of nature. Her second daughter became bedridden when grandmother was sixty and suffered for seven years. This brought all the misery of the world to grandmother. She lost her first child when she was sixty-seven. At that time, grandmother was eighty-four and still going strong. In spite of all the odds she had overcome in her life this one was unbearable, it punctured her zest for life. How could she lose her child right before her eyes? A mother's instinct overtook her courage and her health began to fail. In less than three months she joined her daughter in heaven.

Mother

She was like her father they would say. She was tall and fair with a charming face and expressive eyes. Others often commented that she looked like a film star. Everyone certainly looked twice whenever she dressed up. Charm and good looks are God's gift, if they are complemented with intelligence, boldness, courage, honesty, and integrity then that person is nearest to God's perfect creation. Grandmother was very proud of the fact that she was the mother of such a daughter. Sadly, the only thing mother lacked was a formal education.

When she was married she thought that marriage was a stepping stone to freedom. This thought did not last long. Though marriage was the only option for uneducated, illiterate girls of twelve or thirteen, their age did not match that of grown and mature men. They had to accept and marry whomever the parents felt was right. One had no choice in the matter and had to marry with a mute attitude. Mother tried to reject, and in fact did reject, a couple of men who were prospective bridegrooms. Her parents disliked this attitude. She overheard them complaining to each other about what they should do if she kept on refusing. This made her determined to marry whoever came next. They were not boys but were men who were sometimes prospective grooms for the second time. That is what would give her a bleeding prick. This made her very uncomfortable because she felt it was wrong that this was happening to young girls.

However, her decision did not waver. The third potential bridegroom became her husband. Everyone but she was happy. To her the marriage was not based on her free will but on the necessity of the circumstances. She flowed with time. Time and tide wait for none. She had half a dozen children. When these children would cry, she would cry along with them. Instead of solacing the children, they would immediately stop crying and ask her why she was crying.

As time passed, she realized that bearing further children was meaningless. To her good fortune she was based in the capital city of Nizam. She thought of undergoing surgery that would stop her from having more children. A very unacceptable, innovative thought indeed! Considering the mid-twentieth century's conservative society this thought was bold. She went ahead with the thought by hunting for the right gynecologist with a perfect hand. This went against the wishes of her conservative husband and most concerned family members. She felt that she was the one who would be going through the brunt of every pregnancy. All those who kept wagging their tongues hardly realized her torment. "Those thoughts gave me the inner support and the courage to go in for surgery to avoid pregnancy. This was a rare step taken by people in those days. People scared me with predictions. I went ahead and it was successful. I was happy, but it was at the cost of my husband's anger and I bore the brunt of it throughout the rest of my life. Later we even discussed separation. This did not happen, as by then second marriages were made illegal. And so life continued with my children's future in mind though not peacefully," she recollected.

The fact that she was not formally educated did not hinder

her from doing anything that she wanted to do in life. With her husband working in remote areas, she settled in the city and owned a house, which was very unusual for middle-class people at such a young age. The fact that she did that at such a young age shows her capability with finance management. Her initiative to educate her children at some of the city's renowned schools not only shows her attitude but also her ability to do things on her own in those conservative decades. As for educating herself she successfully completed quite a few private writing examinations. She was good at both Marathi and Hindi. She would subscribe to the then popular and famous Marathi magazines, like *Sthree* and *Kirloskar*, that were based on women's power and awareness.

"All this was not easy," she would say. "It required going through a lot of stress. Convincing everyone else is the biggest task, overcoming hurdles is too tiresome. It is draining, particularly dealing with the conservative minds." This bold and forceful attitude towards life helped her effectively swim through the tides.

Her bond with her only daughter was very strong. Her unfulfilled dream of becoming a singer faded with age. That was really sad. They shared almost every aspect of her life. The daughter was very understanding and sensitive, aware of her mother's roles as an understanding daughter, a disturbed wife, and a caring mother. There was an invisible bond between them that everyone around could feel and understand. Her powerful personality influenced her daughter, and her daughter acquired the qualities of being bold, courageous, and having no fear.

She accepted both chosen and arranged marriages for her children and performed them with equal gravity. She was large hearted mother who valued the uniqueness of every individual. In due course of time, life promoted her to the status of a grandmother and she enjoyed this to the fullest. Her own marriage was a total disaster, a complete mismatch of minds and ideas that resulted in unofficial divorce. After some time to adjust, this brought her much solace. She was comparatively content in her own way of life. She would quote, "Freedom is heaven." Along with other things in life, this brought its own share of invisible and hidden stress, which caused her otherwise good health to fail until she became bedridden. She suffered for seven years. Until the day of her death she could not understand why this happened to her. All of her children, along with their spouses, were totally supportive in helping her out through this time until she reached the shores of life and was engulfed by the darkness of death.

Daughter

She was like a faded object compared to the powerful, towering personality of her mother. Her childhood was as innocent and fresh as morning dew on blossoming flowers. As a child she enjoyed the Almighty's creation in a natural and simple manner. Nature was her friend and all animals and insects were her companions. Her sensitivity toward nature lasted throughout her life. It was like she had imbibed it in her previous lives, or so it seemed since there was no other explanation as to why she dealt with nature in a friendly, sensitive, and caring manner. She was a normal looking, innocent, and inquisitive child, powered with an education from a city missionary school. This education was like adding the required spice to make the dish palatable, delicious, and appetizing.

The golden era of films was at its peak. Almost everyone from every class of society was influenced by the quality of film and music. It was natural that this girl nurtured the secret thought of becoming a film star, a dream that faded as years went by. There was a dynamism in national education after the newly acquired independence of India. She was lucky enough to have a mother who saw to it that the best education was given to her daughter along with her sons. This had a very positive result, and her daughter became a post-graduate in the times when society was still awakening to the idea of education and employment for girls to make them self-reliant. Mother was very particular about this as her experience-based learning taught her that it is very important for a girl to earn her own living and be independent in order to enjoy her freedom and make herself happy.

Being the leader of one's own life, particularly in the area of economic independence, brings much delight and makes one's life meaningful and free. These thoughts were imbibed to the depth of her personality and were very important and helpful over the course of her of life. They led to her success in life. Though married, her education led to her economic independence, a real boon to her already redeemed mind. A very generous heart and an independent personality made her life meaningful. It was like the Almighty, in the form of a life partner, was always there beside her in her endeavors to learn, lead, and live a self-determined, self-regulated, and self-sufficient life. The blessings of her mother left a bright sheen on her life. This bold and courageous lady was there for every part of her life, oozing with the newfound zest for life that was awakening in the women of independent India.

She was naturally inclined toward the stirring, arousing, and initiation of women from all walks of life. This made her content, happy, satisfied, and pleased. She put all her efforts toward this awakening of women, which found its fullest expression in her writing. This brought out her flowing ideas and enlightened her in the process. Writing opened a Pandora's box for her colleagues, and women felt more at ease, happy and pleased that they were not alone in their suffering. The solution for women, who make up 50 percent of society, was found in the form of education and employment.

It is sad but true that 5 to 10 percent of the female population is the target of feticide, infanticide, or honor killing. She was restless to find a solution for society and worked to bring awareness about the value of female participation and the long-term ill effects of marriages based on dowries. She worried about this as though it was her personal domain despite knowing that there is no magic wand and that society must slowly evolve.

One early morning on the highway on her way to work, she saw a huge fallen buffalo suffering acute pain. Some insensitive, stupid, intoxicated fellow must have hit it. She could not tolerate when anything bad happened to animals. She stopped her scooter to see why the animal was not able to get up in spite of its efforts. A closer look revealed that it had been hit on the back part of its spinal cord. She wanted to see the buffalo stand and requested that a few people help, but it was not possible to make the animal stand. They pulled it to the side of the highway and left it there. On her way home in the evening she saw that the animal was dead. It was a sad day for her. She is a very sensitive person who loves animals and tries in her own way to comfort any animal in trouble.

On the subject of the dowry, she rejected all those who demanded a dowry and married a decent gentleman with broad shoulders, a large heart, and no dowry. He was like a godsend and the happiness in her life began with a bang. Her patriotism reached a new height because she married a soldier. She gave birth to a lovely sweet angel, of whom she is still very fond and loves immensely. Her daughter was an angel, a very understanding person, a perfect creation of God, the product of years of her mother's meditation. Life was smooth and adventurous, a combination of contrasts, with her bubbly daughter around filling her life with zest and enjoyment.

This daughter was the center of the mother's smooth and successful life. She performed with flying colors in her academics and was picked up by the best global company, where she met her dream boy. The mother accepted this with an open mind and a large heart, and gave him the green light to marry her daughter. They were married in the traditional way without any dowry, and this was an achievement for the mother because she practiced what she preached.

Granddaughter

In Indian society a granddaughter is the apple of everybody's eye and is loved and cared for by all members of the family, irrespective of their social status. Maximum love is showered on her, specifically from her mama (maternal uncle). If she is the only niece of many aunts she is the luckiest. That is what happened in this granddaughter's case. This is the best thing to happen in anybody's life.

Fair, with curly hair and chubby cheeks, she was the exploring type with a soulful twinkle in her eyes. At the age of two she tried to switch the transistor radio on and off and change the frequencies. She also played only the black and white broadcasts of Doordarshan. One of her photos was chosen by a renowned magazine for its children's section. Her future was full of promise. She never cried or troubled her mother, not only as a child but also as a teenager and beyond.

She worked hard and used her innovative and exploring

skills in everything she did, including her academics. Every time she came out with flying colors. Her fantastic communication skills took her to national level participation from her school--MOCK PARLIAMENT COMPETITION, where they won. She was a dynamic child with overflowing energy; her goal was to reach the sky. She loved freedom, a trait that flowed through her genes and was nurtured and encouraged by her parents. She was a black belt in karate, the art of self-defense, a very necessary skill for girls today to protect themselves. She was an animal lover and always wanted to do good for them.

Her sensitivity toward human beings, particularly her parents and relatives, was her weakness. She put this to use in a most positive manner, supporting herself and learning to live and enjoy life. She worked hard to maintain her economic and social independence. An informed and aware person, she lives a happy, cheerful, and blissful life.

She had a flair for writing, possibly inherited, that she used to express her thoughts and ideas in an imposing manner. When she finished her schooling, she did very well in her favorite subjects, math and science. Her performance in math was outstanding. With grit, determination, and perseverance she completed her post-graduate work at one of the most internationally renowned institutes. From there she took a job at one of the best global companies, which brought her great satisfaction. This was just the beginning of hard work in her career. Her love for independence and the warm, loving guidance and support of her parents gave her immense strength to move forward in life.

Youth is the age when a person is taken by surprise by so many things. In her case, a colleague proposed marriage and she accepted. She made it clear that she would not accept the practice of dowry in her life and marriage. To everyone's surprise, the open-minded boy and his family had the same idea. We joyfully celebrated the marriage with all our relatives and friends and were content. She married in the most traditional manner and will live happily ever after!!

23. On Being Sensitive to Animals

"Until one has loved an animal, part of their soul remains unawakened."
—Anatole France

"Summer is here and it's going to be equally harsh to the animals around us. Kindly do your tiny bit by keeping a bowl of fresh water outside your balcony or garden." *—Consumer Voice*

"No man shall exercise any Tirrany or Crueltie toward any bruite Creature which are usuallie kept for man's use." —Nathaniel Ward

"The concept of being sensitive to animals is ancient. It has been in existence since time immemorial. It prohibited pulling wool off sheep, and the attaching of ploughs to horses' tails, referring to "the cruelty used to beasts," which Ryder writes is probably the earliest reference to this concept in the English language"[3]

Despite different approaches, advocates broadly agree that animals should be viewed as non-human persons and members of the moral community, and should not be used as food, clothing, research subjects, or entertainment.

First, let all humans be informed of the inevitable and eternal cruelty used to compel animals to perform before revenue-paying audiences.

Cruelty to animals is rampant all over the world, whether it is on land, at sea, or in the sky. Appropriate awareness must be frequently brought to people, taking into consideration the experiences and experiments of the past and providing an appropriate vision for the future. This must cover the earlier concepts of understanding animals' physical and psychological pain.

---

[3]http://en.wikipedia.org/wiki/Animal_rights#First_known_laws_prot ecting_animals_in_the_English-speaking_world

This type of awareness can be brought to schoolchildren and colleges to inform a large chunk of future citizens. In turn they will be able to envision a way to save animals from extinction and stop the illegal activities of killing and using them for human benefit.

Human beings are also animals. If one does not accept this then it shows his or her ignorance about nature. If one becomes aware of the facts then one is able to know nature and understand it. If you look into the eyes of any animal, bird, insect, or reptile you see the same feelings that humans feel, whether it is love, fear, anger, or hunger. When all of our spirits are the same and we all have the same feelings, how can we not be sensitive to animals? They are here for their own sake and not for us.

We must be empathetic towards their feelings, and in particular, their fear. If we understand and act accordingly we see immense love and affection in the eyes of each and every creature of the Almighty. They are born here just as I and you are. Like us, they do not know why they are born. They do not know what came before birth or what lies beyond death, just like us. How can we take it for granted that we have the right to trouble, treat with cruelty, or kill a living thing? If we do, how can we call ourselves part of civilized society? How is it that man goes beyond his senses and is not sensitive to the feelings of those born in nature? Understand them, look into their eyes, and empathize with them.

In spite of having common sense and desirable knowledge, people tend to be indifferent to their feelings and carry on with acts of cruelty.

Doing anything with animals for money is the trend of the day. People catch all kinds of birds, to the extent that even sparrows and crows are denied their freedom and kept in captivity until they are sold or die. What authority do we have to do this? Is there no other way of livelihood than troubling the creatures of God? Animals like birds, monkeys, tigers, elephants, and goats are trained to entertain the public and earn money. In India, snakes are made to drink milk on Nag Panchami when we know that snakes live on frogs, lizards, birds, and eggs. This is only to fool people and earn money. Animals are used in circuses to entertain people. How can wild animals be tamed to earn money? When that is done one is working against nature. Animals are used in films and television shows, which is very inhumane.

The planet has become technologically advanced. This simply means that jobs for humans and animals are replaced by machines. It logically means the oxen used for agriculture are replaced by tractors. The oxen, horses, and donkeys used for transportation are being replaced by vehicles. These animals are now jobless. Who will own and feed them, or allow them to feed in the jungles and fields? None of us are because it is a profitless burden. The jungles are being deforested with such speed that there are concrete jungles everywhere. Where will these animals go? Men sell them to the butchers and make money in the process. What an idea! It's not just an idea though, because that is what is being done. Rural people are selling their cattle. The cattle are then transported to cities in a very inhumane, merciless, brutal, ruthless, and cruel way. Though there are rules for animal protection, who can be bothered with them as long as they can be exploited to earn some money. It is harrowing to see these trucks with overloaded animals on the highways. The animals are beaten black and blue to make them listen, bruised during transportation, and are sick and tired and sometimes dead before they reach their final destination, the slaughterhouse.

Slaughterhouses are a hellish environment where the animals' feelings are ignored. Controlling these animals is a hellish task. Their physical strength has to be overpowered and their fear of impending death brings out their aggression as they try to defend themselves. What the sight and the plight of the other animals in the slaughterhouse makes them feel, whether physical or emotional, is beyond my imagination.

Roadside slaughterhouses are growing rapidly and this is a sad state of affairs. It is a product of the human attitude. This craving for animal food is worse now than it was before the birth of Buddha. Has insensitivity replaced mercy, kindness, and a civilized mind? Irrespective of caste, creed, and religion, people are involved in this negative lifestyle. When will civilized awareness dawn upon humans, making them realize that how they treat animals is a reflection of themselves? There is no difference between a wild animal hunting in the jungle and a man killing animals in a slaughterhouse. When will humans stop craving animal flesh and replace it with grains, vegetables, and fruits? The end of this craving will end meat-eating and in turn this will end killing. When can we see peace and happiness replace pain, fear, and terror in animal eyes? End slaughter to bring peace to animals.

Reading is a very good habit that not only improves language but also increases awareness. I love reading but I regret reading this one. In Kerala, in a time long, long ago a man dreamt that a deity asked him to sacrifice one thousand lambs. Since then it has become a ritual performed every year. This is certainly the height of madness. Collecting one thousand animals, overpowering each one, tying them, holding them, and slitting their throats cannot be understood by anyone with presence of mind. On the other hand, there is a man in Mumbai who was the fourth generation in a family of butchers. One day, he had a sort of enlightenment or realization that what he was doing was cruel. He and his wife vowed to stop. He not only stopped but is also involved in stopping truckloads of bulls and cows brought to the city for beef. He does this despite threats to his life. Why does the couple do this? The answer is simple: to see peace in the eyes of the animals and maintain their purity of heart.

Another very inhumane act is to use innocent and harmless animals in experiments for medical purposes, the development of technology, and even in space research. Monkeys and other healthy animals are held in captivity and injected with highly dangerous diseases. When the disease spreads all over the body, the animal is then tested with various medicines to find a cure. Most of the time, the animals die during the process. This also happens when animals like monkeys and dogs are used for space research. The animals are unaware of anything other than its training. As a result, they often die or vanish into oblivion. Sometimes the suffering is unbearable to this helpless creation of God. Humans are solely responsible for such things.

In earlier decades, using animals for entertainment was rampant in both the circus and films. Animals like sheep, birds, horses, dogs, elephants, and tigers and lions were trained to perform in circuses, keeping them in captivity until death. These animals lost their freedom and ultimately died in captivity. This awareness throughout the societies in the world has taken its roots. In India, the use of circus animals has been stopped and declared as illegal with a heavy penalty. Many pockets of lands all over India have been declared National Parks. These areas allow wild animals to live in their natural environment. The very serious problem of animal poaching has emerged, and poachers who are only interested in earning money by selling animal body parts have become rampant. However, the government and animal welfare organizations have become more sensitive to the issue and are working toward ensuring the safety and welfare of these animals.

India boasts about its natural silk and pearls. No one tries to see beyond this to the scenario behind it. Silk is obtained by putting live silk worms in boiling water. Pearls are nothing but calcium deposits inside seashells. They are obtained by killing oysters. We can help animals to live happily by disowning so-called luxury items like silk, pearls, leather, fur, and other items made out of animal parts. The government is doing its best to provide safety to these cohabitants of humans. What is our individual contribution? It is very simple indeed! Discard everything that hurts any animal in any manner and live a clean, pure, and a stress-free life.

The belief that the problems, issues, diseases, and umpteen other hurdles in life can be cured by animal and bird sacrifices is most unfortunate. Animal sacrifice is the most unscientific, barbaric, and absolutely mindless act. It happens all over the world, and it is rampant in all parts of India as well. This wild, widespread, and extensive problem is very depressing and disappointing. Religious sentiments are relevant but sadly it remains difficult to control. The fact that this has been going on throughout the ages means its roots are deep and strong. It will not vanish with the wave of a magic wand. People in every corner of the country must be educated and made aware in order to eradicate this absolutely foolish and stupid belief. It is a slow but sure process. It is the duty of all educated and aware human beings to work toward this goal in his or her small way, to influence people and make them understand the reality of the situation. In rural areas, this deep-rooted, widespread, and senseless belief must be thoroughly uprooted. This can only be done through education and awareness programs.

The most barbaric lifestyle is to not be a vegetarian. It is so rampant and wide spread globally that it cannot be condemned in this manner. Yes, everyone must have been an animal eater in the ancient, uncivilized, and barbaric society of the Stone Age. Today we are supposed to have evolved into a civilized society with infinite knowledge and immeasurable awareness. Therefore our lifestyle is changing as more people become vegetarian. This shift to vegetarianism not only reduces the torture of animals but also brings peace of mind and health consciousness. People are gradually and steadily realizing this and all over the world people are choosing to become vegetarian health reasons.

What are the laws? What can we do about it?

It is against the law to:

Give an animal any injurious substance. It is illegal to put out poisoned food

Prevention of Cruelty to Animals (PCA)

Transport any animal in any manner that will cause him or her unnecessary suffering. This includes loading cows into trucks without ramps and overcrowding the vehicle as well as tying up pigs and carrying them on motorcycles (PCA, Section 11). All violations of Section 11 are punishable with a fine of Rs 100 ($2.00) and/or up to three months in jail.

It is illegal to kill homeless animals. Citizens may only report what they perceive as a nuisance to the municipal authorities. The municipality is required to maintain a pound for animals. Previously, municipalities would kill these animals (mainly dogs) cruelly by electrocution, starvation, and burying alive. After 1992, it became illegal for municipalities to kill stray dogs. The High Courts of Delhi, Rajasthan, Gujarat, Mumbai, and several other states have specifically forbidden the killing of stray dogs and have directed the municipality to introduce a sensible sterilization program instead. The Animal Welfare Board of India has established a code of conduct for municipalities. Failure to follow the code may invite contempt of court proceedings.

Sections 428 and 429 of the Indian Penal Code make it

illegal to maim or cause injury to any animal with a monetary value greater than Rs 10 ($0.18). It is illegal to throw acid on cows (something that vegetable sellers do routinely). The code also makes it illegal for cars to purposefully injure or kill dogs, cats, and cows on the street. Offenders should be reported to the local animal protection group and police station, and a case should be filed under the above-referenced sections. Punishment is a fine of Rs 2000 ($35.00) and/or a jail term of up to five years.

Stray animals may not be used for research. The Rules for Experimental Animals, as formulated by the Committee for the Control and Supervision of Experimental Animals, state that only animals bred for the purpose of research by institutes registered with the committee may be used for experimentation (although, of course, such animals suffer and feel pain just as much as strays or any other animal). It is illegal for any medical, educational, or commercial research institute to pick up stray animals from the street or from the municipal pound for this purpose.

What You Can Do to Help Stray Animals?

When you see a dog or cow being hit or stoned, be sure to inform the offender of the law and get him or her to stop. Should the abuse persist, register a First Information Report (FIR) at the closest police station. Do not become discouraged if the police do not take you seriously at first. In many cases, they may not know the laws pertaining to animals. Be polite but firm.

If the municipality in your area is still cruelly killing homeless dogs, make an appointment with the municipal commissioner. Inform the commissioner that it has been proven that cruelly killing dogs does not reduce their number or the incidence of bites and rabies, and that the courts have ruled that it is illegal to cruelly kill stray animals. The Animal Welfare Board of India has developed a set of guidelines for all municipalities directing the implementation of the Animal Birth Control (ABC) program. If there is an animal welfare organization in the area, urge it to implement the ABC program.

It is illegal for a municipality to round up stray dogs and

drop them outside city limits, as it places them in circumstances likely to cause their death from starvation and thirst. Therefore, you should challenge this cruelty in court.

When you find cows or buffaloes on the street or tethered on public sidewalks, ask those nearby if anyone knows their owner or the dairy where they belong. Inform the owner that it is illegal to allow cows to wander. If the owner does not have enough space to keep the cows comfortable or the means to feed them, file a complaint with the municipality asking that the cows be sent to a suitable shelter. Cows and buffaloes left on the street are often hit by cars or die from eating plastic bags, broken glass, and other trash.

If you notice cows or other animals with burn marks, usually on their rumps, near particular fruit and vegetable markets, it is probable that the vegetable sellers throw acid on the animals to drive them away from their stalls. If there is a market association, approach the head and inform her or him of the law (IPC, Sections 428 and 429). Request that all vegetable vendors be warned against this practice. Inform the police station in the area to keep an eye out for such violations.

When you see an animal knocked down by a vehicle, get the number of the vehicle. Check the animal for signs of life. If possible, move him or her to safety and administer lifesaving first aid. If you can take the animal to a veterinarian yourself, do so. If not, call an animal welfare organization that has an ambulance. Once the animal is taken care of, file a complaint against the offender with the closest police station (IPC, Sections 428 and 429).

If you know of any research institute that uses animals, ask for the source of the animals. If you suspect the animals have been taken from the street or a pound or that the animals are being abused, contact the Committee for the Purpose of Control and Suspension of Experiments on Animals (CPCSEA). In the meantime, file a case with the police.

24. Sri Meenakshi Temple: An Awesome Wonder of the World

Peninsular South India is a unique expression of nature. It is surrounded by three bodies of water, the Arabian Sea, the Bay of Bengal, and the Indian Ocean. The Eastern and Western Ghats taper down to the south and end at the tip of the land. It is a beautiful piece of nature's creation, with hills camouflaged with greenery, and invaluable and incredible plants, roots, and herbs.

It seems as though the surrounding waters are holding the beautiful states of Kerala, Tamil Nadu, Karnataka, and Andhra. These states are spread with temples adorned with incredible, far-fetched, and inconceivable architecture that represent the rich and prosperous ancient culture that had a full-fledged knowledge of the amalgamation of art and science. These structures are a testament to spirituality with their precise, advanced understanding of engineering and refined architectural excellence. The beauty, exquisiteness, gorgeousness, splendor, and magnificence of nature complements the brilliance, superiority, and distinction of the people involved in the construction of these temples. All temples of ancient India are undoubtedly scientifically planned structures that dazzle the most technologically developed scientists of the world. One such exquisitely well-planned structure is Sri Meenakshi Temple.

The origin of Sri Meenakshi Temple at Madurai in southern India goes as far back as 1600 BC. The *puranas* (scriptures) tell us an interesting story about the temple's origin.

The purpose of the *mandapam* (veranda) was to distribute food to people who came from far off places. Now it is used to sell fruit. The beauty, loveliness, attractiveness, charm, and magnificence of the art lies in the micro to macro handling of the stones that were sculpted to tell the tales of those times.

These works of art are still intact and there is no place left empty anywhere on the walls. These artists displayed their devotion, commitment, assurance, dedication, and loyalty through their work that has lasted for ages. The description found in every stone in the temple is self-explanatory.

To conclude about such a magnificent and majestic temple in only a few words is unacceptable, improper, undesirable, and unjustifiable. Sri Meenaski Temple deserves a suitable, appropriate, fitting, and apt appreciation, admiration, and gratitude of the highest order. The expression of the rich, ancient, healthy, prosperous, flourishing, and thriving heritage of the era on the stones and a place built with such magnificent, majestic, wonderful, glorious, and splendid artistic engineering and precision is inexplicable. The art spans from the twelfth through the eighteenth century without effecting the compactness of the structure. This is an amazing wonder that stands as a witness to the reflections of society over the centuries. It is difficult to understand, appreciate, and realize the art and architecture's importance in terms of the fantastic creativity and most pleasing artistic expressions. The artists of centuries ago needed patience, perseverance, persistence, determination, and diligence to bring forth such excellence, fineness, brilliance, and distinction.

The temple needs to be renovated without altering the artistic excellence of the present art. Using the latest technology to bring out and highlight its beauty, make it adequate, up-to-date, and acceptable as one of the wonders of the world in South India. The Temple Trusts and the government can both contribute in order to successfully raise the temple to a level where it is wholeheartedly and unequivocally accepted as a wonder of the world, in line with the Taj Mahal of northern India.

25. A Day Out

It was a strange feeling of relief when they finally had their own dwelling on the outskirts of the city after a quarter-century of a nomadic kind of life. It was a modest, self-sufficient house on a green belt by a state highway with greenery surrounding it. Their dog Snoopy was as thrilled and excited as they were. They adored him and he reciprocated their adoration ten-fold. He was full-grown, ferocious Dalmatian. He was one of their prized possessions and they would not part with him for anything on earth.

Early one pleasant morning she went for a walk with her dog. While they were walking she suddenly noticed that he was restless and making noise. She saw a scooter with three grown pigs tied to it; one was tied lying on the back seat and two were tied hanging from either side. The pigs were squealing loudly, and her stomach churned unpleasantly at the distasteful sound. The man was driving the scooter toward the city, probably to sell the pigs to some slaughterhouse to make a living. She was still thinking about it when a man rode by on a bicycle. The man had tied as many chickens to his bicycle as he could, all hanging upside down. Her feelings were empathetic toward these living things, but she could not convince the humans that what they were doing was wrong. They could not understand her logic and explanations as far as the animals were concerned. The helpless chickens could do nothing but curse him. Even she could do nothing but curse him in the heart of her hearts. To bring awareness about "kindness to animals" and enlighten him was an unachievable dream at that moment because his frame of mind was "the more the chickens, the more the profit."

With a heavy heart she accompanied a friend of hers who was visiting a couple of schools for work. As her friend was busy getting her job done, she was observing the schools and their premises. In the olden days a school was well-ventilated with big and spacious classrooms and huge playgrounds. Today one very rarely finds such places. The classrooms have become pigeonholes with hardly any fresh air or open space. If they are available at all, it is a luxury that only a handful of parents can afford for their children. She was taken aback to see rabbits, monkeys, pigeons, peacocks, and tiny, colorful birds squeezed into cages. This, she was told, was to give the children knowledge of various animals and birds. "Is this the way?" she contemplated. How can the concerned authorities be ignorant of or not bothered by such activities in schools that certainly give the wrong message to children of impressionable age? How can educational institutions educate on the wrong things of life? Logic stopped there.

As she was returning home, she saw a dog badly injured by some vehicle. The dead dog had lived its own life unmindful of radio technology, highway traffic, overpopulation, and the high speed of life before meeting this gory end. All animals have their own reasons to be here just like us. We are nobody to decide on that. She had come under a wheel that had crushed her stomach. All her internal organs, including the stomach and intestines, had come out in a heap through the wide-open mouth. This was an indigestible sight. Adding to it, one of her puppies was going round and round, ignorant of the realities of existence. This touched the heart of hearts within her and gave her an intense feeling of disgust toward mankind.

History tells us that Prince Siddhartha's day out changed his whole attitude toward life and made him a religious teacher in the attainment of nirvana. Her day out makes her wonder how it is that in spite of the wide spread of Buddhism throughout the centuries, which essentially teaches compassion to animals, India is the same old land of insensitive people.

This was her day out. Any takers?

26. A Welcome Reality

It was a very surprising but welcome reality that made a home deep in my heart. To find such a reality happening around me involving sensible, practical, and broad-minded men in this society of oppressed women, I felt a sense of pride, satisfaction, and pleasure at having such open-minded men in our social arena.

Ramesh, being the responsible eldest son, looked after the welfare of all his younger brothers and sisters and made sure they were well settled with jobs and marriages. He is lucky to have a very understanding family with a wife and two grown children. He is a man of values who would go out of his way to help people in need around him. He is a very simple soul. But God doesn't spare such people. He lost his father and mother in Delhi in two separate traffic accidents. Vehicles of all types cause traffic congestion on the roads of almost all cities in India and the results are deadly. One day, as a consequence of mad traffic on Delhi roads, Ramesh got the message that his brother Rhithik had a scooter accident, killing his wife and baby on the spot, but Rhithik survived unhurt.

Ramesh kept his cool and took care of everything and brought his brother to his house. Time is the best healer and it healed everyone's wounds, at least superficially. After a couple of years, Ramesh thought it was time for his brother to marry again. After a brief exchange of views, he placed an ad in the newspaper with all the details and inviting marriage proposals. Among a few responses he found a father's anxious offer to marry his young, widowed daughter with a baby daughter, whose husband had died in an accident. Ramesh answered it, thinking that his brother would get a wife and daughter if everything went well. The two families had a get-together. Surprisingly, without wasting time both the boy and the girl consented. The marriage was performed. The infant found a father. The girl found a husband. The boy found the missing wife and the child. They had another child after a couple of years. Their happiness continued to grow. The father, the brother, and the boy were all men of our society. I sincerely hope we will continue to find Indian men with such simple, clean, and magnanimous hearts.

27. Upholding the Dignity of a Housewife

Housewife is a very complicated word but it overflows with an ambience of cool and peace. Though a housewife is looked down upon, a house is never complete without a housewife; a house is lost without a wife. Without a housewife the husband has no existence in a figurative sense. All this brings out the importance of a homemaker and the essence of a housewife.

A housewife's responsibilities are many. There is no beginning or end. They are infinite. Whether or not she is a working woman, the life of a housewife requires constant work and attention, with patches of rest in between. Looking after the personal, basic needs of her family members requires love, patience, tactics, and above all, the much-needed energy and sacrifice. The woman readily gives all this at the cost of her "self," her desires, her ambitions, and, ultimately, her complete life. Ironically, this is neither appreciated nor recognized and is very conveniently taken for granted. Her invaluable investment of these priceless and precious factors is overlooked and family members in Indian society consider this their privilege.

In reality, the lady of the house is the source of strength and inspiration for the whole family. Her love for all members of the family works as a psychological cushion at any point in time, either in joy, happiness, grief, or crisis. This "love" has its roots in all pervading sacrifices of the lady of the house. Sadly, this fact is either not realized or is overlooked or is taken for granted by others. A housewife is an ignored, neglected, and exploited by other members of the family.

Children are a housewife's end product, and she grooms them so that they will become productive members of society. This stands to be her exclusive and extraordinary contribution: mastering all the arts and skills necessary to run the mini-world that is family. This encompasses society, the nation, and the world at large irrespective of her social strata or geography. By working for her family she is working for the positive, constructive, and productive development of everyone.

In this career of a housewife, marriage is the appointment order and she cannot claim any kind of leave. The work must be done unless she is sick or bedridden. There is no such thing as rightful payment, either by check or cash. She has to slog through old age without any pension. It is a pity that all this is created by male-dominated society. Initially this had a good and positive intention, but later went against her individuality, identity, and existence. That is where the transformation took place negatively. It is a pity that male-dominated society enjoys unpaid women's slavery in the garb of "housewife." This has led to the powerful and unhealthy feeling in the hearts of women that they are doing "a thankless job". Anything she gets in return in the form of love, security, food, clothes, and shelter are the only perks. Her salary is missing. A housewife has no individual standing in the matter of property and ownership. As a result, her psychological instability seeps into the family resulting in frequent squabbles, irritations, and arguments that lead to separation, divorce, domestic violence, neglected children, and suppression; the majority of women tolerate this silently and without question. To bring a halt to this, to erase these negativities, the solution lies in the empowerment of women in a real sense, not in the much-hyped political sense.

Housewives receive no recognition at any stage, from the family level to the government level, with the exception of the meaningless lip service from men at every level of society. The requirements for the empowerment of women in a real sense are many. A housewife's status must be recognized at every level, from the family, the society, and the government. Institutions must be formed that will provide the infrastructure to hold the status of a "housewife" on par with an efficient, skilled, intelligent, and administrative job. This bulky chunk of the nation's strongest primary workforce cannot be neglected. It is high time that a housewife's worth is realized in terms of money. These institutions will cooperate and coordinate by providing information and guidance to this essential workforce. Every housewife must be paid handsomely by the government. Why not? Her contribution in terms of value-based hard work towards her children, who are the future citizens of India, should be recognized. When she is paid remuneration for her services, her self-esteem will increase. She is expected to be the most deserved of all. Financial strength boosts the workforce psychologically. This drastically reduces broken bodies, domestic violence, shattered minds, marital killings, and suicides. Trafficking in women, forced labor, the harsh and stressful concept of "superwoman," sexual exploitation, and forced marriage will all be invariably reduced or disappear. It could be an invisible antidote to today's feticide and infanticide. A female in society will certainly develop a place of esteem from her birth to her death and this will be a wonderful solution to the entire gender problem throughout the globe.

It should be brought to the attention of all caretakers in societies throughout the world to pass a bill to this effect and work in this direction to provide funds, infrastructure, and administrative services through an appropriate system that will be an effective welfare measure. Any positive, practical, and intelligent ideas from all corners of society at all levels are welcome, particularly from empowered women. All government organizations, corporations, and business organizations that wish to contribute in any way by forming and running institutions that uphold the status of a "housewife," who in turn upholds the status of a family and the country at large, should do so because it will be a boon for the development of the nation. Thus the empowerment of women will be fulfilled in a real sense.

28. Nightmare of a Nation

Points to Ponder

Is this a total victory? We have pounded our own land, bombed our side of the Line of Control, lost 398 soldiers including thirty-nine officers, and have twelve men missing in action. Six of our soldiers tortured, their mutilated bodies given to us, 578 army men wounded and disabled. We have spent hundreds of millions of dollars every day for about two months. Is this really a victory as claimed by our army chief and the prime minister?

A father of a soldier who laid down his life wails and puts across this way. Those who failed in their duty, those who are at fault and are responsible for this ghastly and marathon encounter with the enemy, must be identified and dealt with severely, as they are the murderers of our soldiers.

Seema Mustafa, a columnist and writer, is right when she says the talks on Kashmir should be closed. Pakistan should be told point blank that Kashmir is an integral part of India and there is nothing more to talk about. Kashmir should be removed from the agenda of bilateral talks with Pakistan. Talks should be considered only on the condition that there will be no Kashmir involved. It is high time we take this bold step. Why can't we be truthful with ourselves and frank with the deceitful and backstabbing enemy? Any kind of terrorism from across the border should be reciprocated with a firm hand to prevent any further violations.

Mustafa is absolutely correct. To deal with such things effectively we need a nation that is economically and militarily strong. This requires a stable government. To have a stable government we need political representatives who will work together and succeed as a team irrespective of the party he or she belongs to. In spite of having a caretaker government, the people and politicians of our country have proven that they are no less than soldiers if it comes to that. For once, the government and the opposition's contribution to the success of the Kargil crisis is amazing. It is not that they can't do it. They can do anything if it is in the national interest. Every task for the development of the country should be taken seriously as it aims at the nation's well-being. The essence of the conflict is proof that the people and politicians of India are no less than soldiers. Kudos to Prime Minister Vajpayee's patient, firm, and mature way of conduct, and his management of affairs in those critical days of war and aggression. There is no doubt in upholding the people's overwhelming support. This approach should be maintained by all sections of our country, in particular by the government, the politicians, and the bureaucrats, even in day-to-day, routine developmental work.

29. Birthday Wishes

What's with the age that seems to just increase!?
Come on God! Take a break. Spare me please.

Old is you know . . . OooLD . . . not Gold!
I have high hopes, higher aims
Bigger wonders to embrace . . .
I have lots of family and lots of friends
I have a world that never ends!!!

Oh my God! I never realized
I just asked you to take away what is much prized!
Stagnation is not good
I would grow infinitely if I could
Phew! What's with age God . . . seems to just confuse!
One more year added
One more year subtracted
Another bag of experience richer
One more wrinkle poorer
What is perennial is the ever-increasing treasure of good wishes
Please accept one more . . .I wish you all the happiness and
strength in the worst and best of times!

30. Vibes with Vibrations

Vibrations are a set of waves that are the root of a form, living or otherwise. Vibes are the positive compatibility of one set of vibrations with another set of vibrations.

Every set of subtle vibrations has its own individual characteristics, whether in plants, trees, insects, birds, animals, or humans. Any minute change will cause a change in its form, structure, and behavior, and their uniqueness is created. This is nature's way of working toward evolution. Since ancient times, the Vedas have proved that the formative basis of creation is vibrations. The beginning of every formation in nature is a set of vibrations.

In the beginning, these vibrations are in their purest form. They are just positive but as they grow they get corrupted, contaminated, dirtied, polluted, or infected due to external influences. Every baby—a baby plant, a baby lion, a chick, a human baby—is innocent and they vibrate with positivity so that we all fall for their godly innocence, or in scientific terms, their pure vibrations. The purity of these vibrations becomes influenced and contaminated as identity interacts with this creation. No piece of creation is beyond the influence of muddled vibrations. But the silver lining is that it can be dealt with. Negative vibrations can be purified and brought to their original pure and positive status. There are many techniques for this, as there are spiritual men who have committed their lives to learning the knowledge of the Vedas. They guide us with their experiences and put the common man on the right path for purifying his vibrations. The purer the vibrations are in a society, the more positivity and harmony and peace prevails in a society.

This technique is called meditation. There are various methods of meditation that lead to the same goal of redeeming the soul or reverting our contaminated energy back to its pure form. It is an exercise of our consciousness. The energy in each one of us is a set of vibrations that is purified with this technique. It must be learned under the guidance of a guru or teacher, but one should discriminate between a genuine guru and a fraud. Once that is done, one has found a path with a guide. The spiritual (that which is related to the spirit or energy within us) journey is on. Now we need to understand what it does and how it does. What exercise does for the body, meditation does for the mind and the spirit. This is very simple. The energy in us is the subtlest form of our "self." Just like a body gets disorganized with the passage of time, the energy or the self within us also gets disorganized. The way a body gets organized with exercise, the mind and energy get organized with meditation. This energy, or the self, is like the seed of a plant. Nurture the seed, take care of the plant, and it grows. Water the roots and not the leaves for it to grow, blossom, and provide fruit. In the same way, meditate and take care of the subtler form of you, and the self and everything else falls into place.

With meditation the impurities of the mind are thrown out in various ways, depending on the person's constitution of body, mind, experiences, and lifestyle. The vibrations of a self or spirit get organized after throwing away the impurities and even the most agitated mind calms down after meditation. A calm and composed mind is extremely positive in attitude and is able to face any obstacle in life. It is like a body of water that is unruffled, tranquil, peaceful, and quiet. If you throw a small stone into such water you see ripples form and move outward in organized circles. A person who meditates finds no difficulty in facing problems and finding solutions to any frustration in life. His thoughts and actions are organized and sensible. On the other hand a turbulent body of water is like a disturbed mind. A stone thrown into it cannot be traced. A disturbed mind, when faced with any difficulty, cannot act properly to face the problem or find a solution.

Therefore, it is essential that our energy, inner self, consciousness, awareness, or set of vibrations within us, by whatever name one calls it, be purified and organized daily by practicing meditation.

Any meditation technique requires sitting quietly and closing all five senses. The awareness or consciousness or self that naturally tends to come outward should be guided to reverse direction and move inward. As this happens, the accumulation of various stresses that grow like invisible nodules or knots of vibrations get arranged and organized by releasing stress. These stresses are released in various ways in various people. When it happens with the regular daily practice of meditation one finds over the years that the person has overcome irritation, anger, and arrogance. All the negative tendencies of the mind slowly disappear and the person calms down and regains an orderliness of the mind that is reflected in his behavior and actions. This maturity is the result of organizing his set of vibrations or energy or self. Meditation removes the knots in a rope (stressed energy) and smoothes the rope (organizes the energy) to make it useful for anything. A man with organized energy is capable of finding solutions to all the hurdles in life and accepts them in a positive manner.

As a result of regular meditation practice, the orderliness of the subtle level of energy brings orderliness to the brain and nervous system, which in turn brings balance to all the other systems in the body, like the circulatory and digestive systems, which result in the organized performance of all the organs, tissues, and cells. This helps to maintain the organized functioning of every part of the body with its secretions held in balance. Over the course of time a person realizes that major and minor health complaints have automatically disappeared without the use of medication. The logic is simple. The imbalance that resulted in health complaints has now been provided with balanced, organized and pure vibrations, and the body has started functioning properly because the hurdles or blockades created by stress have been organized or melted away. As a result the person begins to feel healthy and cheerful.

The purification process continues with regular meditation, the disorganized changes into organized, the disorderliness transforms into orderliness, and the purest form of energy manifests itself in good health, good behavior, a glowing face, and a positive social acceptance in every walk of life.

31. The Himalayas and the Heights

Fantasy means dream, fancy, and vision, and apply all these to the imagination of the Himalayas, one of the highest peaks in the world, and you will have the urge, the desire, a wild emotional surge to visit, see, experience, understand, and get familiar with this magnificent natural creation of God. Something goes faulty in the imagination if one has not visited it. Therefore, it is very important to see it in person in order to understand this wide stretch of bulging earth. It provides a solid and bountiful means of imagination to writers and poets. This massive natural structure provides unlimited, boundless, and infinite food for thought.

The Himalayas spread from its highest peaks in the western range to the sloping eastern range. The height reduces oxygen levels as you move upward. Whether one is walking or traveling in a vehicle, the journey is a tedious one. Once you get tired of it you crave the plains. The terrain, landscape, topography, and environment are not as easy as the plains below. The terrain is hard and difficult. One has to be born there to get used to it. The landscape is full of ups and downs and rarely has paved roads. It has a difficult topography that makes living difficult, tricky, and complicated. The top of the peaks are packed with snow; these snowy peaks bring cold weather all around the chain of mountains. This kind of chill and snowfall is more common on the western ranges and high peaks, along with Mount Everest. If one is living in one of these areas, like Kashmir, it is difficult to face the whole season of snowfall and one wants to be back on the plains. This weather is less intense on the sloping ranges of the Ladhak region. With change in elevation the weather conditions also change. The next area of these mountain ranges is occupied by Sikkim, Nepal, and Bhutan on the Indian side, and the highest plateau, Tibet, on the other side. Kanchendzonga, Nandadeep, and Nandakot are some of the highest peaks on the sprawling, extensive, rambling, and expansive mountains found here. These mountains are carpeted with either stones or greenery except in the cold season when you find the divinity of the mountains expressed by vast sheets of pure white snow. This snow forms the unending, continuous, perennial life-giving source of water on the mountains as well as on the plains below in the form of the sacred and divine Ganges, Yamuna, and Brahmaputra Rivers, which flow on the holy, blessed, and sanctified land of India.

These mountain ranges motivate every aspiring soul to satisfy their strongest adventurous urges. The mountains invite children, the young, and all adventurous souls to come and try their hand at walking, riding, and driving on these mountains, to experience the thrill of climbing to various heights, challenging nature in its toughest form, taking the tricky path, overcoming the demanding landscape, riding successfully over the exigent texture of the tough terrain. This is not easy, but it has challenged people throughout the ages to try to conquer this part of nature.

These mountains are static, unlike the dynamic oceans, yet it is tedious to move around as one either has to climb up or down, which is monotonous, tiresome, wearisome, and mind-numbing. To climb the rocky mountains is not easy. To face extreme weather is not simple or trouble free. Driving up or down requires a lot of practice and skill, and it is a demanding job. The western ranges are known for their ice-capped peaks that makes the weather bitingly cold. The region is cold for six months and the other six months are like pleasant summer without the prick of the sun. The eastern ranges are comparatively smaller in height and face a typical pattern when it comes to seasons. Here there is no summer season. There is either chilly winter or pouring rain. Each season lasts for six months. Overall, whichever part of the Himalayas we talk about, about the mountain range is beautiful and bountiful with the sprawling mountains, the snow-capped peaks, and the intermittent rivers in the valleys.

Here one finds a treasure of forests, thick with peculiar trees that are specific to each region. As usual, money-hungry people are working vigorously to make a fast buck by fiddling with nature. This is unfortunate because it strips the majestic, grandiose, magnificent, splendid mountains and erases the most valuable species of trees and plants. Since time immemorial it was known that the Himalayas were abundant with all kinds of plants and trees that are not found anywhere else in the world. There needs to be special mention of the trees that are unique to their region, the medicinal plants and herbs that are used for various purposes down on the plains. *The Ramayana* states that Hanuman flew to the Himalayas in search of the herb *sanjivini* to bring back Lakshman to life. These mountains are the storehouse for these unique, exclusive, and inimitable trees, plants, and herbs that are invaluable and useful.

That people have built towns and cities on and around these mountains and valleys gives proof to the fact that in spite of the difficult terrain, the complicated topography of these mountains attracts and catches the fancy and attention of people. There are all kinds of settlements, from Srinagar in Kashmir to Darjeeling in west Bengal to Leh in Ladhak, to Sikkim, to Tibet, Nepal, and Bhutan in the northeast. There are various forms of culture residing in these sprawling settlements that are centuries-old. The people are simple, lovable, and uncomplicated. Buddhism is the most accepted faith apart from Islam and Christianity.

The highlight of these people is that they are close to the ultimate creator and his representative, nature. Their belief in Buddhism is evident in their closeness to the natural environment. Their innocence lies in the acceptance of nature as it is and they revere it in its natural, rugged, and harshly magnificent form. This is intermittently reflected on these mountains in the form of monasteries (*gompas*). These are religious structures that overflow with expressions of their faith. Rhumtek Monastery is one of those nestled on the mountains.

All along the Himalayas there are cities and towns and they have become a hub of tourist attractions for the beautiful, stunning, eye-catching, and heart-throbbing scenery of deep green valleys and White Mountain peaks. Tourism is the main occupation of these mountainous cities and towns. The well-developed cities like Srinagar, Katmandu, Gangtok, Kalimpong, and Darjeeling are the renowned central destinations of these regions.

32. Journey through Galaxies

I was a different self before I was born. I could feel my existence. I suppose I was not visible to mortals. I could not be touched, smelled, seen, heard, or spoken to. I did not exist mortally, but my existence was absolute. Absolute existence is mass-less, light and movable, and a part of space cradled me. There was no shape, no size, no weight; it was an absolute experience of existence though mortally I was nonexistent. The realization of my existence without in fact existing was a great feeling. But what was I? Where was I? Why was I? These were the questions that could not be answered. My awareness was not mature enough to realize the reality of nonexistent existence. My depth of enquiry and curiosity led me to believe that this is a state of being that is invisible but there is an absolute reality in its depth.

The form was formless. It was matter in its plasma form. In other words I would say it was a formless existence of a nonexistent form. I could feel the power in me that the mortals of today would love to feel. I suddenly realized the most powerful, invisible energy flowing in me, faster than the fastest internet, precise and accurate in performance. The power was so strong that I had ideas of moving through the hottest of the fiery galaxies and the coldest of frozen places in far-off space. The idea transformed into a forceful, dynamic, and vigorous urge to move through them. I, like any normal being, succumbed to the urge and began to move. This submission and surrender held a store of surprises. I realized that the power I had was incredible. Would I be able to control it? It was fantastic to experience that speed of movement. It was very smooth and I was in control of maneuvering myself through live and dead parts of celestial existence with speeding directionless meteorites hustling past me left and right. Slowly and steadily I became aware of my super-fantastic, improbable, incredible, and unbelievable capabilities. As this awareness dawned on me, my confidence to enter the most dynamic space stations of the Almighty's creation multiplied immeasurably and I could feel the surge of energy that I acquired from these celestial bodies. The closest was the sun that nourishes the earth itself. As I dived out of my home I could see bigger and smaller satellites that play an important role in mortal beings' lives on Earth. As I was trying to maneuver through, the speed of light entered me and that was a very accelerating experience. I was super-activated by the surge of energy and could pick up speed that was incredible. My performance power was supreme and it ruled and urged me to surge through with unbelievable acceleration. Once I stabilized this influence I could concentrate on the space objects left, right, and center. A sudden beam of super sunlight made me aware that I was among the planets of the universe. There were the big and small planets with their satellite moons clinging to the planets like babies to a mother. An awesome sight indeed! These amazing, breathtaking sights became common as I sped further. It reminded me of the song, "Space is so startling Venus is there and Mars; Space is so startling not just the stars."

Apart from the small and big planets of our sun, the stars sprinkled all over were amazing. As I passed the siblings of Earth, I wondered whether any of the planets was as fertile as our home. It seemed futile to look for a fertile planet as the signs or evidence of life anywhere near them was nil. A sudden jerk made me realize that I had come into a different arena that threw me out further into space. It was incredible, amazing, and awesome to see billions of big and small shining stars moving around. The ambience was mysterious yet very lively and moving. The unimaginable, inconceivable, and unthinkable size of these live, celestial objects was astonishing to see. Their eye-catching and blinding glare was part of the boundless and absolute structure of creation. I passed through limitless and abundant universes like our own, each with its own sun, small and big. These suns have their own families with their planets and their satellite objects.

There was no means of keeping tabs on the time I spent to reach these places. There were no human routines of food, water, and shelter as I was in my absolute form. I could not rest anywhere as I was under the influences of the pulls and pushes of these spatial bodies for my survival, and to accept that was to move forward. Space was so crowded with the incredible number of stars and meteorites that most of the time I was hit by these small and big meteorites. They seem like stones on Earth, coming with such speed that they can disturb the rotation of the earth, but when they hit me, I could hardly feel the brush of it and they would pass through me. My absolute form probably saved me from collisions. In a fraction of a second I realized that I was on a huge, enormous, vast, massive stretch of stars that made a way for me. It looked like an amazing and astounding conduit of star lights stretched with a diamond-studded carpet to welcome me to the still more spread out world of unbelievable creation.

I traveled through the members of our universe to other universes and from the Milky Way to the world of galaxies. I sensed gleaming, shining, burning and cooling fire. Burning ashes in an unimaginable and unbelievable mammoth form were sprinkled all over space. From the most disorganized creation came the most organized manifestations from the unmanifest. I wondered at times, "Was it a futile search for life in a brimming world of balls of fire? Was I going through the essence of transformed reality?" My hopes were not dashed. I remained hopeful, positive, optimistic, encouraged, and upbeat.

It was fascinating to wonder about the existence of life on any of the celestial bodies. The calculations of logic, fantasy, and imagination led me to believe that life exists away from earth, but there was no factual evidence that I could carry back home. As my absolute form wandered with electronic speed, covering innumerable light years every fraction of a second, my "self" sensed the existence of different kinds of life under various other conditions that suited each planet's peculiar and unique environment. A sudden realization dawned on me that it was time to take a U-turn and head back. It was exciting to go through the same experience of speeding through the twinkling, shining, and bright celestial objects. As I was returning it was heartening to see my home universe with the familiar sun and planets. Within a fraction of a second I realized that I was in sight of Earth, my "home sweet home." It was pleasant and relaxing to be back.

Sumathi Kulkarni

Then I had to move on earth sailing by the boat of karma. I found myself in the womb of my mother transformed from my absolute self into the mass of cells and tissues that form a fetus and a human. The whole journey was like a lost dream. It was the absolute experience of an absolute self but I have no business remembering all that is out of the realm of human existence on earth. Not remembering anything turned out to be the beginning of my journey on Earth. Thus I found my next form as a baby.

33. Black Forest

It all started with a howl
No one knew what was that yowl
The dogs barked, the insects creaked
The koel cooed, the birds chirped
The jingle and the tinkle, the rattle and the jangle
Were all there in a hurry; was there a flap and a flurry?
The man yelled, screamed, and shouted followed by
Clink, clank of the ringing bells
The clatter was there with a fluster and a flutter
That led to a heartrending shriek, followed by
The noise of thud and jangle
This brought a loud roar that brought in
Slop, blub, and a bawl
This led to a cry, weep, whimper,
The thud, the smash, the bang and the clang
All in one, adding to that
There was a mew, a croak, a holler, a wail
But then there was also one who was singing.
Was all this in a jungle, a black forest of noise?

34. Journey of Life on the Waves of Emotion

A human being is a bundle of emotions. All these emotions are stored in his permanent memory bank. In many cases they are either inherited or acquired. Whatever the case may be, every human being rides on the waves of his or her emotions as they sail through life. The beginning is when a baby cries at birth; perhaps this is the tragedy of arriving on Earth! Is that entering with a negative emotion? Probably not. It may just be preparation to overcome and accept the pain of life. What is an emotion? A set of subtle vibrations, a response to outside stimuli, or a physical response guided by the inner self. A person moves through life on a wave of emotions.

Emotions are varied. They are named. Anger, fury, rage, resentment, annoyance, irritation, despair, misery, desolation, hopelessness, anguish, gloom, dejection, depression, sadness, grief, sorrow, heartache, pain, woe, happiness, pleasure, joy, glee, bliss, delight, contentment, gladness, and cheerfulness are all emotions that we as humans experience on a daily basis. They are of two kinds, positive and negative. Positive emotions are the most organized and negative emotions are the most disorganized in terms of their set of vibrations. The temperature and heat of negative emotions are of a higher degree, whereas positive emotions work under a very suitable level of heat and low temperature. A positive response is a cool, sensible response based on an organized set of vibrations. Therefore a cool person is never agitated while an agitated person's behavior is based on the stimuli of excess heat.

The flexibility of behavior is a result of flexibility in these sets of vibrations, which in turn are based on heat, temperature, and their compatibility with the situation, environment, and the response to stimuli.

Love is the most engulfing, spontaneous, and omnipresent emotion. It is a powerful, smooth, accepting, and working emotion that makes everyone magnetic and attractive to one another when they ride on this emotion. It works on all animals also. They respond naturally and positively. Once that compatibility is obtained between human and animals, there is no need to be scared by the wildest of animals. They respond positively, absolutely, and completely. This flexibility of behavior is either hereditary or acquired with positivity and practice. When mingling with people, it helps with cooperation, coordination, and cohesiveness, thus contributing to the success of any task at hand. This emotion shuns or stops negativity from entering both parties concerned.

Human beings are not a perfect creation of God though sometimes it seems to be so. Flaws find their way in. Sometimes tempers rise due to environmental situations that lead to anger and irritation, sometimes jealousy, selfishness, envy, or hurt lead to acts of violence when emotions cannot be contained. It can also be the other way around. Any happy event arouses positive feelings that get translated into joy, glee, gladness, contentment, satisfaction, and pleasure that are then interpreted and transformed into actions of celebration. One should understand that every feeling, positive or negative, has its own set of vibrations.

The emotions of large groups can have a powerful impact and act as a force of change in a region or society. Patriotism, mass movement against suppression, or transforming the development of society are among these types of feelings. In scientific terms, this is simply the collective positive vibrations of people acting upon society with a forceful, dynamic, vigorous, and influential integration of mass vibrations.

Whether it is an individual or a mass activity, everything in life rides on the emotions. To conclude, it is essential that these vibrations are under control and used sensibly to bring a positive end. These vibrations can be controlled through the practice of yoga, which is a scientific process of organizing oneself in terms of cleansing the disorganized nervous system, throwing out stress, and bringing pure energy, aura, and brightness to calm the soul and allow it to sprout positivity.

35. A Rainbow Beams Across

Truth and purity last with wholesomeness and transparency
No one can antagonize the white against black
Sincerity counts, honesty and genuineness are valued
And respected with earnestness.
It attracts people like a magnet
Goodness prevails in individuals or masses
To work wonders galore with decency, integrity, righteousness,
To be wonderstruck with spotlessness, clarity, and
Simplicity that radiates spreading shafts of light across
To bring the like-minded together
To work for the people, the society, and the country at large
Devoid of all negative energy
The positive to float and charge and recharge
Unity against the institutions sacred, but made a hash of
Or underutilized and bungled, to bring out the real essence
To bring in meaning and work with upbeat actions.
To reach out to the people with glowing changes
For harmony, accord, unison radiating from every corner
That is what Anna was for, with the masses following.

36. The Bygone Mirth

Creation is female in gender. Everything in this creation is created. Therefore, one who creates or gives birth is a mother. This is why the mother is held in high esteem. Mother divine is the creator of everything. She takes the lead in being worshipped as the invisible power. Every female part in creation is strong, flexible, enduring, accepting, tolerant, manageable, and divine. This can be seen directly in nature, anything can have these qualities. Earth is female. The endurance and tolerance it shows is commendable, laudable, worthy, and admirable. In its own way, the earth is productive, supportive, creative, fruitful, dynamic, prolific, and useful. Although it suffers the abuses that are showered on it and yet the earth remains busy in its positive efforts to continue its process of creation.

It is said that God created Mother Divine because he could not be everywhere. All the qualities that are present in her are present in each and every mother on Earth. Whether we are talking about humans, sea life, birds, animals, or insects, the naturally acquired motherly instinct is displayed in their creative job of the growth and evolution of life. There is no comparison to it. The human species carries it through generations without questioning. It is an integral part of evolution that every baby requires the care and nurturing of its mother in all stages of growth. So the motherly instinct is in the female of the human species.

The concerns, the needs, and the attitude toward women is in question. In spite of being a sacrificing mother, a giving sister, a good wife, and a concerned daughter, females are being abused and ill-treated. According to the UN, every year 750,000 girls are aborted in India. Abortion rates are increasing by 80 percent; the Indian states of Punjab and Haryana lead this trend. Statistics confirm that one third of the girls born survive until their fifteenth birthday.

Society's attitude, poverty, backwardness, and an unaware and uneducated population are the culprits.

The consequences girl children being thought of as a disadvantage, a drawback, or a shortcoming for the family and society are grave. Due to this narrow-minded, negative, inappropriate, and biased thinking, the society is sliding into an abyss. This void is increasing day by day as families find out the gender of the unborn baby in the womb and abort the female fetus, kill female infants soon after birth, throw them in garbage bins, or leave them in the train stations and bus stands. It is also leading the parents of these unfortunate female infants to sell them for meager sums of money. This is a very serious problem. When it comes to the census, the last few decades show very disheartening revelations of numbers of the female population in terms of gender ratio.

There is reluctance in seeking medical aid for girl children, as there is no money and if there is any, it is used for the boy as he is supposed to support the family later. Spending money on a girl's medical aid is not beneficial. Boys are sent to schools and extra attention is given to their education because parents think that girls are not in a position to provide because they will marry and go to the other family. Their earning goes along with them. Young girls, on the other hand, are asked to take care of their siblings while both parents go to work for daily wages. It is a sad state of affairs. Women are treated as second-class citizens not only in families but also in this male-dominated society and the nation at large.

"Frailty, thy name is woman," Shakespeare articulated four hundred years ago. Shakespeare's universality is based on his use of universal truths. This is no exception. It has been two decades since 1990 was declared the Year of the Girl Child. The disparity in the treatment of girls is massively increasing every day. The last two decades reflect feticides, infanticides, biased treatment at home, poverty, unaware parents, early marriages, low nutrition, anemia, lack of education, dowry menace, and forced abortions. This craving for boys has had a grave effect on the census. The gender ratio between male and female is declining speedily. The censuses of 1991, 2001, and 2011 verify the fact.

The rampant abortion of female fetuses reflects the depth of the problem. It is the result of the prevailing thoughts and ideas of the existing society, regardless of class and creed, that spreads the length and breadth of India. Developing technology is used negatively by mischievous elements with the clear motive of making money and getting richer quick. The technology that provides knowledge of the gender of the fetus inside the womb encourages the idea of getting rid of the female fetus while it is still in the womb. Women are motivated to go through with the abortion by force, coercion, and being convinced that a girl child is a liability for the family. These narrow-minded people play a proactive role in persuading and influencing this idea. This is prevalent in the upper and lower middle class, who believe in the advantages of having sons who will earn money and bring in an alluring dowry that will increase the comforts of living. Though it is an attitude with low morals, it is rampant, widespread, and uncontrolled in the majority of the middle class.

The working class has a different story. Whether they are rural farmers facing day-to-day difficulty or migrating laborers to the city, they are faced with poverty and cannot fetch one square meal a day. They do not have room for a girl child in the face of scarcity, shortage of food, and no source of earning a dignified living, which makes them abandon the infant on the roadside. The chief minister of Tamil Nadu, Ms J. Jayalalitha, has introduced a plan where parents can drop the infant in the cradle outside Shishu Vihar rather than abandoning it, and these children will be looked after and taken care by the state until they become economically independent and able to lead a life of dignity. The idea is excellent and the best part is that it is working well. All the other states and central governments can adopt this idea with all its sincerity.

A girl child is treated with bias when it comes to food, nutrition, health, education, and family support, and this is well-known. That the bias begins with breastfeeding is shocking. The mother is of the same gender. How can she either forget this or not understand it? It is the natural duty of the mother to treat a daughter with the same standards as a son. The middle class is aware of this and the practice is taking a downturn, which is a good sign. One finds that most of today's fathers dote on their daughters and stand like a solid pillar of support for fulfilling their dreams in education, careers, or marriage. This shifting trend in society is a positive development among the upper class and some of the lower working and business classes.

The problem still persists among the working class. To some extent it can be controlled through free and sincere education, economic support to the parents of girl children, attractive and appropriate incentives to families with daughters to dissuade them from feticide and infanticide. This will not only decrease these acts of violence but will also bring value to girl children and their importance in the development of a nation. The problem here is the insincere government and its employees who satisfy their greed with the money that is meant for these schemes so it does not reach the people who deserve it and to whom it belongs. There is no dearth of government schemes for the elevation of these unfortunate girls but the hurdle is the system that allows the misuse and mishandling of the budget allocated to these programs. This acts as fuel for the already burning society and rubs salt into the wounds of the poverty-stricken, uneducated, and unaware families who only find relief in this violent attitude toward girl children.

In spite of the United Nations providing the Convention on the Rights of the Child, which include the fundamental rights of survival, protection, and development, what is Indian society reflecting on at this point in time with particular reference to girls? With all these ideas around, it is we as responsible, answerable, and accountable participants in society who are to blame for our children's lives. Abandoning girl children and killing the instinct of creation is interfering with and intimidating nature and nature is going to work accordingly and is going to boomerang appropriately when we lack the number of females for procreation. The huge gender ratio gap is going to create an enormous void in making matches and society will face a tremendous deficit of females, which will lead to massive chaos in society. This kind of discrepancy will lead to gender insufficiency. Let us take an oath to Devi, the most powerful goddess Lakshmi, to work toward warding off the evil of looking down upon the girl child.

After attaining puberty girls are forced into prostitution. This is the easiest way to make money to satisfy their hunger, which is their most basic need. Girls are unwillingly pushed into it by both their mother and their family, and the innocent and ignorant child succumbs to it through no fault of her own. Once into it, it is very difficult to get out, thus encouraging the negative phenomenon in society. Girl trafficking is another menace of society where one finds girls in rural areas being kidnapped or sold by their parents at a very young age, in their need and greed for money. Trying to stop this is a challenging predicament of enormous magnitude and dimension. Creating awareness is the major task in dealing with the unequal status of the girl child.

The tradition of dowry has an honest origin, but has been utilized in a selfish and greedy manner and become mandatory in marriage, which in turn creates difficulty for the marriage of girls. This unreasonable attitude of society creates many problems for the family of the girl to be married.

This tradition is no longer appropriate in the present evolving society where the girls are educated and work on par with boys, predominantly in the middle class. It has been legalized that a girl or family who is the victim of dowry can place a complaint and get a redress in their favor. This is a positive sign. The negative side is that it is still going on despite people's awareness of the law. Nevertheless, a large chunk of today's younger generation is overriding this aspect. However, there are still boys who are influenced by the typical Indian traditions of their parents and family.

Alongside many women's welfare organizations, the government's contribution to solving these problems is tremendous and this is verified and established by many laws in favor of women. Some of them are:

Sexual harassment: Half of the total numbers of crimes against women reported in 1990 were related to molestation and harassment in the workplace. "Eve teasing" is a euphemism used for sexual harassment or molestation of women by men. Many activists blame the rising incidents of sexual harassment against women on the influence of Western culture. In 1987, the Indecent Representation of Women (Prohibition) Act was passed to prohibit indecent representation of women in advertisements, publications, writings, paintings, figures, or in any other manner.

In 1997, in a landmark judgment, the Supreme Court of India took a strong stand against sexual harassment of women in the workplace. The court also laid down detailed guidelines for prevention and redress of grievances. The National Commission for Women subsequently elaborated these guidelines into a code of conduct for employers.

In 1961, the Indian government passed the Dowry Prohibition Act, making dowry demands in wedding arrangements illegal. However, many cases of dowry-related domestic violence, suicide, and murder have been reported. In the 1980s, numerous such cases were reported.

A 1997 report claimed that at least five thousand women die each year because of dowry demands, and at least a dozen die each day in "kitchen fires" thought to be intentional. The term for this is "bride burning" and it is criticized in India. Among the educated urban classes, such dowry abuse has reduced considerably.

Child marriage has been traditionally prevalent in India and continues to this day. Historically, young girls lived with their parents until they reached puberty. In the past, child widows were condemned to a life of great agony; they shaved their heads, lived in isolation, and were shunned by society. Although child marriage was outlawed in 1860, it is still a common practice.

According to UNICEF's *State of the World's Children 2009* report, 47 percent of India's women were married before the legal age of 18, with 56 percent of those from rural areas. The report also showed that 40 percent of the world's child marriages occur in India.

Domestic violence: Incidents of domestic violence are higher among the lower socio-economic classes. The Protection of Women from Domestic Violence Act of 2005 came into force on October 26, 2006.

A well-known karate master demonstrates by saying that if your husband is a violent person, give him a punch in the stomach and then hit him in the groin. That will solve the problem. Well, he is right I suppose!

The average female life expectancy in India today is low compared to many countries, but it has shown gradual improvement over the years. In many families, especially rural ones, girls and women face nutritional discrimination within the family, and are anemic and malnourished.

The maternal mortality rate in India is the second highest in the world. Only 42 percent of births in the country are supervised by health professionals. Most women deliver with help from women in the family who often lack the skills and resources to save the mother's life if it is in danger. According to the 1997 UNDP Human Development Report, 88 percent of pregnant women (age 15–49) were found to be suffering from anemia.

Family planning: The average woman in rural areas of India has little or no control over her reproductivity. Women, particularly women in rural areas, do not have access to safe and self-controlled methods of contraception. The public health system emphasizes permanent methods like sterilization, or long-term methods that do not need follow-up, such as IUDs. Sterilization accounts for more than 75 percent of total contraception, with female sterilization accounting for almost 95 percent of all sterilizations.

It is heartening to see that society is evolving gradually but absolutely. Today's women face complicated and complex challenges. With education, a job or career, marriage, a home, childbearing, and child rearing, women have to face up to these challenges and fight it out to deal practically and be a winner in every area. Though it is not easy, today's women are trying and succeeding in many cases. This requires super energy for these unavoidable tasks. In most middle class families, the silver lining is the father cooperating in the initial stages before marriage. Today's husbands have realized their role, position, and responsibility in childbearing and child rearing, and are aware of the father's share. That is how the challenge of childbearing and child rearing are to some extent is eased by the husband's help. Packing a child off to day care at a young age to make it easier for the working parents is depriving the child of its experience of childhood. In the rat race of employment and earning money children are losing their childhoods. The disappearance of joint families adds to the agony.

Nonetheless, the solution to the problem of girl children lies in a multifaceted handling of the issue. If the family works toward it at the grassroots level, supported by NGOs, social societies, and nonprofit organizations, all topped with legalized governmental support, this will undoubtedly work wonders in increasing the pace of evolution in regard to the issues of girl children. It is an extensive and complicated path. However, we have a sure shot at success if we have perseverance, grit, and determination.

37. Shades of Bravery: Did It Happen?

It was a routine day on the mountains of the Himalayas, in the valley of Jammu and Kashmir where I was commanding a unit in one of the remote areas. The soldiers of my unit were a heterogeneous lot belonging to various parts of India who were here with a purpose, a sacred one at that. One wonders what motivates them to be on the borders and sacrifice their lives for the nation when the people in power are busy feeding their own bulging bellies and doing whatever it takes to become wealthier. What a contrast in the attitude and commitment. One is prepared to die for his country; the other is selling his country. One is brimming with values and the other is selling his ethics, ideals, and virtues for money and pleasure. One tries to live within his limited means and the other's greed has no reins. A soldier's sacrifices are absolutely meaningless and insignificant to a public representative or bureaucrat who is an expert at lip service, who is more involved in making his own life comfortable than working toward his commitment to his country.

Though these thoughts sometimes overtake me, it was my obligation to fulfill my duty instead of digressing into my thoughts. It was mandatory to see that every boy of my unit was on the alert, to be on his toes at all times, otherwise it would be detrimental and damaging to my boys and me. The call of duty is top priority and it must be performed regardless of whatever other undertakings there are. In this sense it was a routine day for us; the regular activities of the soldiers on the post were carried out in a disciplined manner, keeping our strategies in view against the continuous surging of militants. Anything could happen at any time. It was only the vigil on our part that would keep us alive or else we would succumb to the destructive tactics of the invisible enemy. In the rigmarole of preventing this kind of unexpected event there was a message from home about the death of my mother. It was a numbing experience. It took some time to come out of the stressful routine duty to a completely different state of mind and the news for which I was not prepared. Nevertheless, it was my obligation to accept whatever comes my way and move accordingly. My request for leave was unquestionably sanctioned and I prepared myself for the journey home from the Himalayas to the Vindhyas in the south.

Early the next morning, I decided to leave with my QRT (Quick Response Team). As I was passing through the most infested area of militants I heard a very familiar kind of disturbance in the area as a couple of militants were hiding in a house under the cover of the civilian population. As this area was under my command I could see my adjutant with a team of soldiers fighting it out. The area was completely cleared of people. It was cordoned off to prevent any escape of the hiding militants. As I noticed this I could not travel further. In the army it is the officer who leads the soldiers and not the soldiers who lead the officer. The officer motivates the team of soldiers to follow him and his orders.

There was absolute silence on both fronts. There was no firing from the militants or the army. That was a tricky situation. Who would begin first? When there was no firing I moved further into the house in spite of my adjutant asking me not to. I knew it was my duty to lead as a commander and I could not go against my conscience no matter what the consequences were. As I moved there was firing from the militants' end and an appropriate response from the soldiers followed by chaos and a downpour of bullets from all sides. In this mayhem I tripped and fell to the ground, but I was still moving. I was crawling further toward the militants' hideout inside. This was a booster to the already charged soldiers, who moved ahead with multiplied force and enthusiasm. Suddenly, the adjutant realized that the commanding officer, that is, me, was not visible. He panicked and ordered the whole party to stop firing and look out. Within minutes there was lull and in spite of the army stopping the onslaught there was no response of any sort from the other side. The first order from the adjutant was to search for the commanding officer. There was total silence and inside I could see one militant dead and another injured. Adjutant felt a sigh of relief when he saw me unharmed. That gave him the confirmation that the whole operation was a success though a couple of soldiers were injured and arrangements were immediately made to send them to the military hospital after initially treating their wounds. After providing the required instruction for the follow-up activities, I began my journey home to a totally different kind of setback on the home front.

I wondered whether I would be able to take it or not. I was my mother's darling, and she was everything to me. The thought of losing her touched the deepest chord of my heart. It was very difficult to experience. I wished that no one would have to face such a thing though I knew nothing would change with my wishing. This personal loss of mine engulfed, overwhelmed, and swallowed me up as I neared my home destination. The successful operation of duty was left behind; it did not make any sense when it came to losing a loved one at home. I had seen deaths in so many different contexts during my service, but was not equipped to cope with personal loss. But life has to move and we have to move with life. That's what I did. It was like a bad dream that never ends. I had to stop it and I did that very successfully. Today I wonder if all this really happened.

38. Female Is Divine!

The Vedas speak of Mother Divine, I speak of reduced
femininity of mine

Oh mother, you are revered, you are worshipped

I am destroyed, eliminated, and exterminated

What an irony that we both are same

But for the society it is a selfish game

To have a boy and to discard a girl

Is like owning a spike and toss away a pearl

Mothers and fathers say they want a male

To further their ancestors' trail

The more the boys the less the girls

The social problems go in whirls

Man is at his peak of working against nature

Trapped by the shortsightedness of being a creature

Who cannot look beyond self-gratification.

The female is a divine, celestial, heavenly incarnation.

She finds herself among mortal waste in a heap of garbage

Or left to fend for her without care like a rotten cabbage

What makes these mortals do this?

How does it matter if it is hers or his?

Is it the wealth, the name, the honor, or the mean stance?

Or is it bringing the liability by chance?

How can you and I be a part of unevenness?

If I am one you have to be the other

Oh, Divine Mother

Nature will play its part to bring in a chance

To put in everyone an even glance

To smooth the waves, to pacify greed

To work and to work only for the need
To extend a hand to the one who tries
To build only nature's desires
A female is Lakshmi, wealth and prosperity
Also Kali, most powerful, symbol of wreck.
This would certainly hit back
If dishonored and demeaned, debased and shamed
Bringing indignity, humiliation, and debasement
But then it's just a matter of time
A matter of healing a maimed mind
It will rebound, this dwindling number,
A question of man getting up from slumber
To realize and act for the mother, sister, daughter
To let live, be a part of creative earth and heaven
Be treated like you oh Goddess, as holy and divine.

39. My Pets

I don't own them, they are around me,
Varied in number and of invariable variety.
They are from the wild, but not wild,
I don't tame them; but they are mine!
They are like an innocent child working on their way,
I am at ease with them and vice versa.
The long lovely cobras breaking in,
The chirping birds of rainbow hue,
Squeaking squirrels, mewing cats, screaming peacocks,
Rabbits showing at dusk, visiting bandicoots,
Frogs big and small hiding from snakes
The unusual sight of a mongoose, a monitor lizard
Big wild rats appear rarely,
The big fat cat looking for a rat
Crowing crows looking for food
A rich conglomeration of the Almighty's
Versatile creation, big and small,
All colors, all sizes, and all shapes
Making the world a place for living together,
Lizards yellow, brown, green, wrapped in camouflage
What's happening? They're all in race and rage
They are looking out for their prey and food
It's being part of the food chain and not for blood.
One seeking the other for survival
Matter and energy passed on from one species to another
It's nobody's fault for they are they and we are we
They are meant to be what they are
We are meant to be what we are

They accept us with all reluctance
To our overbearing attitude.
Why are we not sensible enough
To accept them as they are?
They hurt us only if we do harm.
We hurt them even if they don't
How selfish, how mean
When it comes to it man is without sheen
Man's intelligence has gone to his head
He is overridden by such a callous stance,
Melts, humbled, and becomes meek with a simple glance
They touch the core of my heart
They teach me "the living art"
To love, be merciful, kind, compassionate.
Empathize with them, they are yours.
Be sensitive and shower love
And you can never be friendless.
Try at it; you will be healthy in body and mind,
Unknown bliss engulfs you at their sight
Love swells your heart, you feel one with them.
The more you give, the more it overflows,
I can vouch for it as they are my true pets.

40. Home Sweet Home

Home sweet home, no place like home,
Back by evening that is where we come
To find peace, comfort, and calm,
To have the best of grub, safety, and haven.
There was the cave, dark and dingy,
Early man craved it, a refuge.
It was a bolt hole that brought shelter
And a secure place for his stalked food.
Man evolved, cave evolved, created a new
Hut with straw, stems, bamboo, and mud.
Cattle around with a dog's bark and a cat's meow
Nature supported to grow into a shed.
A forward step to build an **abode**
Strong with stones all around making one into many.
It was cool and clean with a sturdy floor
Seemed man was happy or was it greed to the core.
The numbers expanded, families grew,
Villages sprouted everywhere,
Result of the comfort, luxury, and harmony,
That grew into towns and cities spread in agony.
People overtaken by greed,
To forget the necessity of need.
Mafias encroached the land,
Houses propped up in band.
Science brought in new concrete and cement,
That made all a slave to this torment.
The jungles were intruded and infringed upon,
The towns spread, the cities stretched.

The commodity called land
Unfairly and unjustifiably was in demand.
But the earth cannot swell for a man to dwell,
The houses began to grow vertical.
It was a newfound idea that spread fast
That did not demand a land vast
The swelled population lived in pigeon holes
Man was proud and happy at his new roles
But then one day the whole apartment collapsed,
Roofs caved in, the walls crumpled,
The earth shook, the land slid,
No one could assess where the error hid.
God was great, no one was hurt,
Babies and elders, men and women
Were grateful though in their grief there was a spurt
But they all believed that in this lay a lesson.

41. Knots of Thoughts

I was both neither deaf, dumb, nor blind.
I was aware of the stench of hard work.
The soup of life smells good,
Only when garnished with an aroma of spice.
It is not easy to become stinking rich.
Smell is a sense, a sense of smell,
One needs to smell out trouble,
Smell out corruption, work through,
To reach out to the sweet smell of success.
It is the fragrance of roses I love,
It is a smack of reek and the odor I hate,
It is the stink of garbage, the stench of sewage
That puts me off.
I adore the fragrance of flowers in the fields,
Perfume made of bouquets of flowers,
Scent of body mist and spray.
A whiff of niff, Odor hum repel me,
Throw me miles apart, but life is not only the scent of roses,
Full of thorns and spikes, pricks and barbs.
The learning is done, shortcuts none,
Pass through pong and reek, if I need to success seek.

42. The Flow

Childhood is a bliss that knows no bounds
To play, to search, hunt, investigate, and explore
To seek out and rummage around.
It is the age of self-learning through
Touch, taste, seeing, hearing, and feeling
The inner layers of soul.
The earth is moving,
Time is moving,
Change is the funda of life everywhere
Why else would childhood stop?
The child grows, the mind grows
And the change occurs and the volatile
Teenage engulfs the soul.
Exploration and investigation change into Experiences to
enrich the learning
Through follies, ups and downs
Sense tries to prevail in the turmoil
Of hormonal secretions
The teenager bows down to nature.

And a youth is formed, moulded by the environment
Dreams are fresh, blood is hot, and the urge is at its peak
Is fueled by actions and reactions that
Teach toleration, understanding, empathy,
And to take the road to evolution,
That makes a complete human.
But then that is not the end.
Dreams are fulfilled, dreams are halfway,

Dreams are shattered or dreams are dissolved in the mirage.
Learn to face the facts of life
Whether happiness or sorrow
When that happens, a sense of achievement smiles.
One never realizes that this phase,
Here one is at the tail end of life,
Old, haggard, with various complaints,
With a pouch of medicines,
Near and dear ones on their way into the unknown,
And I, waiting for the dark day to take me into its fold
From where the flow takes on a new cycle.

43. Flowers

This is the land of flowers
White, orange, yellow, blue, purple, big and small
With lovely aroma and fragrance
That touches the inner self to bring out liveliness.
Flowers are for Gods to be decorated,
Flowers are for women to be adorned
In their lovely long beautiful hair,
Flowers are to cheer up people through gifts,
Flowers are to decorate the *pandals* of marriages and functions
The lovely jasmine, rose, lilies, poppies, lotus,
Saffron and peacock flowers
All waiting to be grabbed and used for various purposes
Known for their variety and beauty
Play a significant role in the ecosystem as well.
The smell arouses the spirit in us,
The scent activates the soul in us,
Aroma builds a positive aura around,
Cologne can quiet the restless self,
Perfume seeks to bring in the bonding.
Such magic the flowers shower
Such mystery descends with flowers
So delightful these flowers are
Such enchantment they create
Such is the soil of India where I am proud to be born.

44. The Dark Way

The dark way is a lonely way where
One's own voice is heard in the noise.
The dark way is where one sees one's own
Visions confronting to come to the forefront.
The taste of this lonely way is as bland as
The insipid blandness itself.
The dark lonely way does not only touch
But engulfs one into its darker folds.
Complete lonely dark way is anosmia Devoid of the ability to
smell.

But then nature's contribution is always
Blossoming with beautiful external influences.
The sun, the clouds, the moonlight, the stars, the greenery,
The chirp, the tweet, the squeak, fragrances, aromas
Transform the dark way into the bright, lively sights
With visions varying in color, hues, and brightness.
Sense of hearing is all about vibrations
That put in pleasing rhythm and beat
To bring in the melody onto the dark lonely way.
The soothing touch, the caring touch,
The familiar touch, the hard touch, the soft touch,
Work wonders in curing the darkness of lonely way.
The smell, the fragrant aroma enlivens the brain cells
To make the thought process brighter
To brighten the dark way of loneliness.

45. Let Us Rise

Things are murky, confused,
Overflowing with filth and garbage
Let us grope, delve, rummage,
Organize and rise above this.
There is external mess, internal turmoil,
Punches coming from all around,
Let me take them, soften
My spirit and rise above this.
The head is going haywire,
Overdose of thoughts getting knottier
Wonder how does it all end, but
Let me loosen these knots and rise above this.
Cheer up my soul, it's all a part
Of the entire play of the Almighty!
Does someone like that exist? Wonder,
If so wait with patience, and rise above this.
Time and change, powerful tools
Those make us laugh or cry
Let's laugh, let's cry and cleanse ourselves
And strengthen our spirits and rise above this.

46. My Trip to a Haveli

It was a very enjoyable journey. We were all in a singing mood. Adding to it there was a very gentle cool breeze. Monsoon drizzles showered like the smiles of a hesitating and shy bride. Flowing clouds played hide and seek in the sky with an ancient fort as the background. All these things made our picnic to one of the rural areas, a remote place in one of the districts, all the more pleasant. Once we reached the place, the fact that we were attending to the serious business of education vanished from our minds within no time.

It was an old zamindar's haveli converted into a school. The couple that managed it were the zamindar's descendants, Non Resident Indians (NRIs) who returned to their native place with a noble purpose. The people of the village had served them and their families for generations. This realization had dawned upon them and it was time for to return the favor. This was in the form of education for the village children. A noble thought and a good reason for homecoming. An applaudable initiative indeed!

Playing in the Folds of Nature

We were here to give a helping hand in fulfilling their aspirations. It was a proud moment for all of us. We found ourselves watching the deprived children find a place to be a part of the developing country in its speed to become one of the superpowers. The management had arranged for us to meet with the students, teachers, and parents. It was very impressing to talk to them. The parents were carpenters, barbers, farmers; all were skilled workers of the village. We were awed at their awareness of the world despite being in a remote village. Can you guess what they asked for? They wanted their children to converse in good English. It was a reasonable demand. They were completely just in asking for that, or else their children would be left behind. The teachers' enthusiasm was obvious both inside and outside the classroom. They were presentable, soft-spoken, energetic, and proactive. They were mentally prepared for any kind of advice on being a better teacher. An ideal teacher keeps abreast of learning throughout his or her career.

Zamindar's Haveli: An Abode of Learning

There was a big difference between these rural students and city students. We were completely taken in by their peaceful attitude, soft but confident approach, aspiration to learn more about everything, and their self-discipline as compared to the city kids who have become entangled in the tempestuous waters of competition and stress. We did not find any teachers shouting or students screaming during breaks, which is the accepted norm of city schools. We sincerely wished this kind of atmosphere could be transferred to every school in the city. We were doubly impressed when they told us that a girl was selected at nationals in archery and a boy was selected at state level. They were sent on to an appropriate Institute both for training and studies. This is no less of an achievement than any of the city schools.

Marching Ahead with the Global Village

The management deserves kudos for their initiative and their work for a noble cause. This is an instance where we witness that thoughts can be transformed into action in the form of a rural high school, with support from the RDF (Rural Development Foundation). It is our sincere wish that the management tastes the fruits of success in their noble mission for a social cause.